You'll Never Guess What *We* Did in Gym Today!

You'll Never Guess What We Did in Gym Today!

More New Physical Education Games and Activities

Kenneth G. Tillman
and
Patricia Rizzo Toner

Illustrations by Patricia Rizzo Toner

Parker Publishing Company, Inc.
West Nyack, New York

© 1984 by

PARKER PUBLISHING COMPANY, INC.
West Nyack, New York

Library of Congress Cataloging in Publication Data

Tillman, Kenneth G.
   You'll never guess what we did in gym today!

   Includes index.
   1. Physical education for children. 2. Games.
I. Toner, Patricia Rizzo,   II. Title.
GV443.T566 1984   372.8'6   83-22071

ISBN 0-13-977075-5

Printed in the U.S.A.

I wish to dedicate this book to my wife, Dee, and our four wonderful children, Karla, Darcy, Dana, and Kai. Karla, Darcy, Dana, and Kai have participated in all types of movement activities, and their play and sport activities have provided countless hours of enjoyment for me as a participant and as an observer.

Kenneth G. Tillman

I would like to dedicate this book to my husband, Jess, my son Danny, and to my dear friends, Mary Lambert McCaffrey of Holland, Pennsylvania, and Barbara Snyder of Richboro, Pennsylvania, who have faithfully tested many of these activities in their physical education classes.

Patricia Rizzo Toner

How This Book Will Spark Your Physical Education Program

Every physical education program needs a spark now and then. We have written this book to provide ideas that you can use to generate enthusiasm in your classes. Actually, we go beyond ideas and give you concrete suggestions and over 325 practical games and activities that you can use in your physical education classes immediately.

We know that you will be following a curriculum that has been designed for your school. The activities included in our book are planned to fit in nicely with existing curricula. There are suggestions and games that are appropriate for every unit in a K-8 physical education program. You will find activities that will challenge, and ideas that will not only make physical education more enjoyable for your students, but will also provide the stimulus that all of us teachers need to maintain our enthusiasm for teaching.

Some of the activities in this book may seem significantly different from the activities found in traditional physical education programs. We have deliberately included these activities. Give them a chance. It is our bet that you will soon become a convert. Remember that we have only included activities that meet accepted objectives of physical education. You will find that innovative activities are just as effective as the more traditional activities in developing skills, promoting fitness, and contributing to social and emotional development.

Do you need to break away from your usual class routine? Let this book be your springboard. You will find that our material can easily be adjusted to fit ages five to fourteen. In fact, we have found activities and ideas included in this book effective with pre-schoolers and high school students.

You can use our material in a variety of ways. Incorporate it into your regular curriculum or set up a series of mini-units based on the games and activities that we explain. You can also apply many of our teaching ideas to your present program to add variety and provide an innovative touch. One of our goals is to assist you in using your creativity to expand the world of your students. The contents of this book make this goal possible.

The eight chapters in this book are diverse. They will meet a broad range of the needs of physical education teachers, as well as classroom teachers, or playground supervisors. Flexibility is a distinguishing characteristic of both the format and contents of this publication.

There are certain times during the school year that are particularly challenging to teachers. Rainy days and holidays always pose problems. We have provided specific aid for these times. Dance is an activity that scares many physical education teachers. We have provided assistance to allow you to incorporate a viable dance program.

Chapters 1 and 2 contain almost 100 games and game modifications that can be plugged into your existing physical education program. Chapter 1 is devoted to team games and is divided into indoor and outdoor games. Some of the games are planned for large classes with more students on each team. Chapter 2 is a good complement to the first chapter in that it provides new and unique skill activities that place a premium on individual action. Activities range from frisbee variations to roller skating to golf modifications.

Chapter 3 highlights dance. The material is presented to make it possible for even the hesitant teacher to provide a challenging dance experience. Dance is viewed as a natural extension of the basic movement program found in elementary physical education programs.

Chapter 4 contains a wealth of material for the physical education teacher to use when teaching in the classroom. This is also an extremely important chapter for the classroom teacher who wants to supplement the scheduled physical education program or to provide movement activities that will reinforce instruction in other subjects. This chapter covers activities that correlate with other subjects as well as unique fitness and skill activities and team and group games.

A change of pace characterizes Chapter 5, and suggestions rather than specific games constitute the format. The ideas can be used by any physical educator and provide changes that will keep your program operating at a stimulating level. The accent in this chapter is on changing your teaching approach and instituting new activities that will capture the imagination of the students.

Rainy days and holidays are frequntly trying days for a physical education teacher. Chapters 6 and 7 are written specifically for these occasions. Rainy days need special activities to overcome the characteristic student restlessness, and holiday seasons need to capitalize on the excitement and anticipation that builds up in the students. Many spirited games are provided for rainy days, and theme games found in Chapter 7 add sparkle to each holiday season.

Motivation is the key to any successful physical education program, and the final chapter is devoted to this very important ingredient. Various motivational ideas are developed to permit you to select those that can be totally assimilated into your teaching and those that can be used as needed during the school year.

Our objective in writing this book is to provide resources that will result in more children excitedly saying to a friend, a teacher, or their parents, "You'll never guess what *we* did in gym today."

Kenneth G. Tillman
Patricia Rizzo Toner

Acknowledgments

To Dee Tillman for typing the manuscript and for her helpful support as this book was written.

To Jess Toner for his valuable contributions and suggestions.

To the Health and Physical Education graduate students of Trenton State College, Trenton, New Jersey, who provided many of the ideas incorporated into this book.

To the students and Physical Education faculty of Council Rock Intermediate School, Holland, Pennsylvania, who tested many of the activities presented.

To Mr. Charles "Chick" Cosover, elementary physical education teacher in Teaneck, New Jersey, whose innovative individual pupil activities for fitness and skill development found in Chapter 4 will provide fun and inspiration for both teacher and student.

Contents

5   *This Sure Is Different!*   145

Over 30 Change-of-Pace Ideas

6   *Raindrops Keep Fallin' on My Head*   157

40 Activities to Brighten Your Rainy Days

7   *Happy Holidaze*   177

47 Ways to Make Your Holidays Dazzle

8 *I Can't Wait to Go to Gym Today* 213

Motivational Ideas to Keep Your Students Enthused About Physical Education

Index 225

1

Wow!
Who Invented This
Game?

Over 50 New Team Games for Indoor and Outdoor Enjoyment

Games have a universal appeal to children of all ages. Each country has certain games that become standard games for its children. Ethnic groups have games that are characteristic of their cultures. Neighborhoods in our major cities provide intriguing examples of games that develop to reflect the physical surroundings and life styles of the children. Different geographic areas have games that evolve due to the influences of cultures of the areas as well as the type of terrain and climate. It is because of this strong appeal of games that this chapter has been included in the book. Even though children enjoy playing familiar games, they also love to try new games. This chapter provides new games that will allow your children to use many skills from games that they have played previously. Thus, they are able to succeed in the new team games and gain the enjoyment that comes from team competition.

Team games have special appeal to children in elementary grades. We have included team games that can be modified to fit the ability and interest levels of your children from kindergarten through all the elementary grades. These team games give your students a chance to participate in games based on fun that provide maximum participation for every student.

These games are ideal to give variety to your classes. There is nothing better to spark interest than a new game that provides a different challenge and a unique approach to a game situation. Many of these games are modifications of games that your children have probably played before. Excitement is generated as your students experience a different way of playing a game that might already be familiar to them. They also have the opportunity to learn new skills and further develop their movement capabilities.

Many of the games in this chapter have been designed by innovative teachers who have used them to give spice to their classes. You will find that your students will enjoy trying different games when they find those new games challenging. They bring a new dimension to your students' physical education experience. These games have been used successfully in both physical education classes and recreational activities.

The activities are divided into outdoor and indoor games, although many can be played both indoors and outdoors. In some cases slight modifications in game rules, playing implements and field dimensions will be necessary.

But now, full speed ahead. Let your children experience the fun of new team games.

OUTDOOR ACTIVITIES

SOCCER-CROQUET

Object: To develop soccer dribbling and passing skills.

Equipment: Soccer ball for each player; croquet stakes and oversize wickets. (Wickets can be made from broken hula hoops, from other materials or an improvised wicket can be made from two traffic cones.)

Description:

Croquet is played using a soccer ball. Croquet rules are followed.

Variation:

Croquet can be played with field hockey sticks and balls. Regular croquet wickets are used.

SIZZLE PLATE BALL

Object: To force players to think before reacting, and move clockwise around bases

Equipment: A rubber base; four cones; rubber playground ball.

Description:

The class is divided into two teams with one "batting" and one in the outfield. Cones are the bases and are placed about forty-five feet apart to form a square. The rubber base is placed in the center of the four bases and is called the "sizzle plate."

The only person covering a base is the person on the "sizzle plate"; otherwise, everyone is in the outfield.

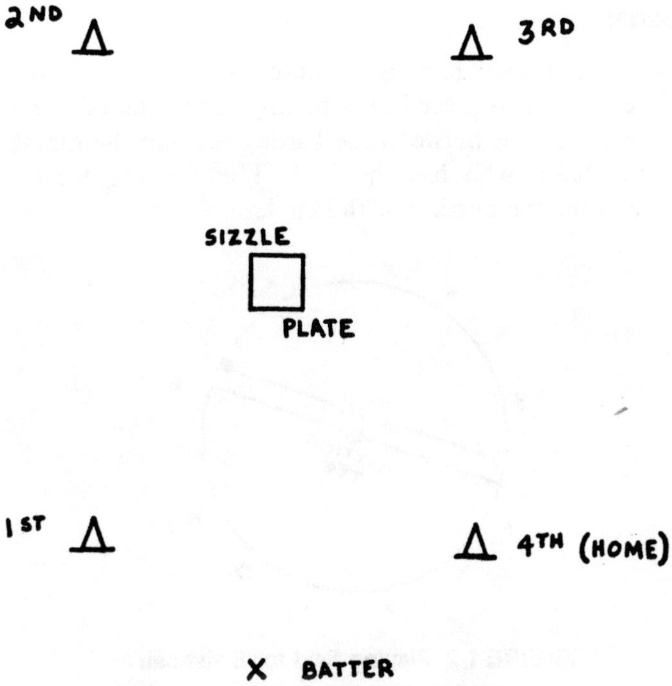

2ᴺᴰ △   △ 3ᴿᴰ

SIZZLE

PLATE

1 ˢᵀ △   △ 4ᵀᴴ (HOME)

X   BATTER

FIGURE 1-1. Position of base for Sizzle Plate

The "batter" kicks the ball and runs left to first base. The fielders retrieve the ball and throw it to the person standing on the "sizzle plate." When that person catches the ball, she yells "sizzle." If the runner is not on a base at that time, he is out. The next "batter" kicks the ball and also runs to first base. There can be any number of runners on a base at one time. Any runner who is off base when the player on the "sizzle plate" yells "sizzle," is out. A caught fly ball is also an out. Three outs constitute an inning.

A run is scored when a runner reaches fourth base.

SWISHBALL

Object: To use skills of hitting, throwing, running, passing, fielding and team work.

Equipment: A flat bat or paddle; tennis ball; batting tee; playground ball.

Description:

A circle eighteen feet in diameter is used for playing this game. A tennis ball is placed on a batting tee in the center of the circle. A batter stands between the batting tee and the member of the fielding team who has the ball. The fielding teams take positions around the outside of the circle.

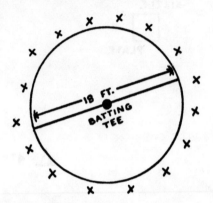

FIGURE 1-2. Playing field for Swishball

The fielding teams attempt to knock the tennis ball off the tee and end the batter's turn at bat. The batter protects the tennis ball by hitting the playground ball as far as possible. The batter then runs to the outside of the circle, touches the ground with the paddle, and runs back and touches the tee with the paddle. A run is scored each time the tee is touched, and the batter yells out the cumulative team score each time. The fielding team retrieves the playground ball and again attempts to knock the tennis ball off the tee. They may pass the ball around the circle to get an open shot.

All members of a team have a turn at bat each time their team comes up to bat. Each player gets to bat until the ball is knocked off the tee.

WIDE OPEN FOOTBALL

Object: To score touchdowns by passing the ball.

Equipment: A football for each game.

Description:

The ball can be moved forward only by passing. Each team is given six downs to maneuver the length of the field. A down starts when the ball is snapped and does not end until the pass receiver is touched with two hands. Every player is eligible to pass or catch the ball, and the ball can be passed forward at any time and from any position on the field. The number of passes thrown during a down is unlimited. The defensive team takes possession on every incomplete pass at the place where the passer threw the incomplete pass rather than at the line of scrimmage or where the ball landed.

THROW-KICK-RUN

Object: To score runs before the opposing team knocks down three cones.

Equipment: A football; two bases; two cones.

Description:

The game is played on a large grassy area. Each player on the offensive team kicks or throws the football and then runs around

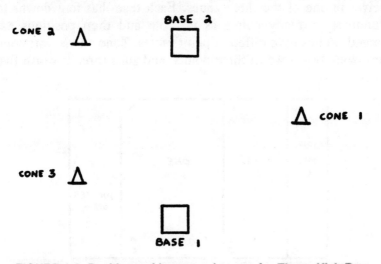

FIGURE 1-3. Positions of bases and cones for Throw-Kick-Run

both bases as many times as possible before the defensive team can retrieve the football and knock down the cones in sequence. A run is scored for each trip around the bases completed before the cones are knocked over.

Variations:

1. Increase the number of cones and/or change the locations of the cones.
2. Require the offensive team to use a designated form of locomotion when going around the bases.

THREE-ZONE FOOTBALL

Object: To have the quarterback pass the ball to a receiver in one of three zones.

Equipment: Football.

Description:

There are two offensive players and two defensive players in each zone. The quarterback has five seconds to throw the ball to a receiver in one of the three zones. Each team has four downs to accumulate as many points as possible and then positions are changed. Zones have different point values. Zone one is worth one point, zone two is worth three points, and zone three is worth five points.

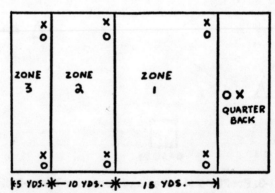

FIGURE 1-4. Field markings for Three-Zone Football

The defensive team tries to prevent the offensive team from catching the ball. On pass interference, the offensive team is awarded the points for the zone. If the defensive team intercepts the ball, the teams switch.

MIXED-UP BALL

Object: To add a novelty element to kickball and keep players alert.

Equipment: Kickball.

Description:

Regular kickball rules are used except that the batter and runners must run in the direction the ball is kicked. For instance, if the ball is kicked to the left of second base, the runners and batter run the bases in a clockwise pattern. If the ball is kicked to the right of second base, the movement around the bases is counter-clockwise.

Each player on the team bats, and then the teams switch places.

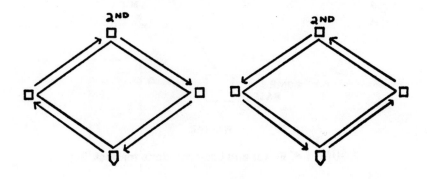

BALL HIT TO LEFT OF SECOND BASE.

BALL HIT TO RIGHT OF SECOND BASE.

FIGURE 1-5. Direction of runners when ball is hit to the left and right of second base

JOCK BALL

Object: To score as many runs as possible before the defensive team can knock over an Indian Club.

Equipment: Wiffle golf ball; tennis racket; tennis ball; football; basketball; large and medium playground balls; baseball bat; wiffle ball bat; wiffle ball; batting tee; rubber home base; three Indian clubs.

Description:

Three Indian clubs are placed on the ground to represent first, second, and third bases. The defensive team has a person at each Indian club. The batter stands at home plate, and the other members of the batting team form a straight line parallel to the foul line.

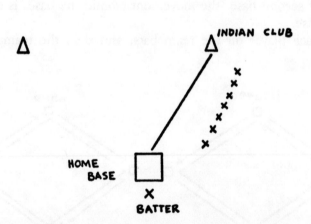

FIGURE 1-6. Player and base positions for Jock Ball

The batter may choose any combination of equipment with which to bat. (Tennis racket and wiffle ball, baseball bat and playground ball, etc.) As soon as the batter hits, he runs around the Indian clubs and touches home plate as many times as possible before an Indian club is knocked over by the defensive team. While the batter is running the bases, the first person in the batting team line runs around the line as many times as possible. One run is scored each time the teammate completes one revolution as well as each time the batter crosses home plate.

The defensive team tries to knock over an Indian club to stop scoring by the offensive team. In order to knock over the Indian club, all members of the team, except the person next to the nearest Indian club, must run to the person picking up the item that was batted and line up in a straight line. The item is passed between each person's legs to the next person. The last person throws to the person next to the Indian club. This person throws the item to knock down the Indian club. If the Indian club is missed, members of the defensive team must pass the item between their legs again before throwing at the Indian club.

SOCCER-BASEBALL

Object: To develop dribbling and trapping skills while playing a modification of baseball.

Equipment: Two soccer balls and four cones.

Description:

Boundary cones are used for bases. One soccer ball (Ball A) is placed three feet to the left of the home cone and the other ball (Ball B) between home and first. (See Figure 1-7.) One team is at bat, and the other is the fielding team. The first batter kicks ball A into the field as in kickball. The batter then runs to ball B and, using a soccer dribble, goes around the bases without stopping. Upon reaching home, the batter kicks the ball into the cone.

At the same time, a fielder traps ball A and kicks it to the first baseman who traps the ball and hits the first base cone. Passes are then made to second, third, and home in that order.

It is an out if the catcher hits home before the batter. A run is scored if the batter is successful. After two outs, teams change places. A batter touching the ball with hands is out, and a run scores if fielders use their hands.

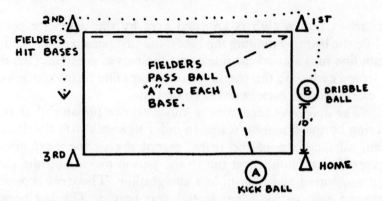

FIGURE 1-7. Diagram of playing area and placement and movement of soccer balls

PRO BALL

Object: To have students use plays they see when watching a professional football game.

Equipment: Football for each team.

Description:

Have students watch a pro football game on television and diagram plays they see. Have each class team practice the plays they have diagrammed and then demonstrate three running plays and three pass plays to the rest of the class.

Variation:

1. Have teams use the plays when playing flag football.
2. Follow the same procedure after watching other pro sports on television.

FIELD DODGE BALL

Object: To circle the field base and return across the home base line without being hit with the ball.

Equipment: A large rubber ball, soccer ball, or volleyball.

Description:

Two teams are formed with one team starting as the running team and the other as the fielding team. A half-inning is completed when all players on the running team have had an opportunity to run a designated number of times. The teams then switch positions. The running team lines up behind the home base line and the fielding team members disperse over the playing area.

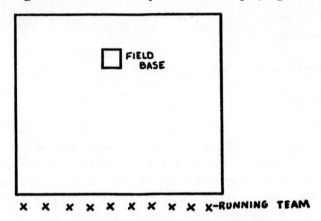

FIGURE 1-8. Playing field for Field Dodgeball

The game begins when the instructor rolls the ball onto the field of play. Two runners must immediately try to circle the field base and return without getting hit with the ball. A legal hit is between the shoulders and the knees. A fielder may run to get the ball but must remain stationary when holding the ball. A fielder may either throw the ball at a runner or pass the ball to another fielder who is in a better position to throw at a runner.

There always must be two runners on the field. A runner who is hit legally must raise an arm high in the air to signal the next person on the team to start running. The tagged runner then returns to the end of the line as rapidly as possible without interfering with other runners or fielders. A runner crossing the home base line is also a signal for the next player to start running.

Two points are awarded for each run scored. A player foul results in one point for the opponents. Teachers should designate fouls before play begins. Types of fouls will vary with age and skill level.

Variation:

A game may be played in two or more time periods. Members of a team must run in sequence, and the team continues to score as many runs as possible within the time limits.

ONE PITCH SOFTBALL

Object: To speed up play and get maximum action when playing softball.

Equipment: Softball; bat; and bases.

Description:

Most of the rules of softball are used. Exceptions are that each team furnishes its own pitcher and each batter gets only one pitch to hit. A ball missed, fouled, or not swung at is an out. Each team stays at bat until every player has batted. However, the bases are cleared after every three outs.

Variations:

1. Permit a designated number of outs per inning.
2. Permit each batter to have one swing rather than one pitch.

DROP AND KICK

Object: To kick the ball far enough to be able to score a run.

Equipment: Kickball.

Description:

Two teams are formed with teams alternating kicking and fielding. The objective of the game is to kick the ball, run across a marker line and return to the home line without being hit with the ball.

The kicker must be hit while running the danger zone—between the marker line and home line—in order to be out. Kickers have the option of trying to score on their kick or waiting

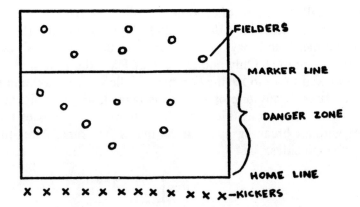

FIGURE 1-9. Field markings for Drop and Kick

for another team member to kick the ball. A point is scored for each player who crosses the home line. The kicker starts the action by dropping the ball on the ground behind the home line and kicking it on the rebound. If a runner is hit in the danger zone, the teams change positions. Every player on the fielding team must then cross the home line before being hit by the ball or the kicking team gets to remain at bat.

Variation:

Give the fielding team one point if a player catches a fly ball with one hand. Score two points if the kicker returns to the home line without being hit.

CALIFORNIA KICKBALL

Object: To score more runs than the opposing team.

Equipment: Five bases; one kickball.

Description:

Five bases are set up as shown. Rules are similar to kickball with some important changes. Outs can be made only by tagging a player or group of players, or by catching the ball in the air. The players do not have to run, but may wait as long as they wish on the bases. There is no limit to the number of players on any base. Any time the ball is kicked, one, some, or all of the players on a base may run to the next base but *any* and *all* players leaving the base *must join hands* and may not break apart or they all must sit down (counts as one out). Only one group may leave the base when the ball is kicked to avoid having one player followed by another a few seconds later. If any one of a group is tagged, all must sit, but it counts as only one out. However, if a group of five crosses home plate, without breaking apart, it counts as five runs. After three outs, change sides.

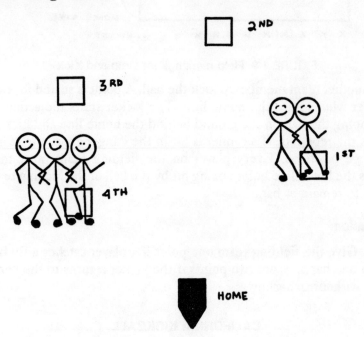

FIGURE 1-10. Field diagram for California Kickball

INDOOR ACTIVITIES

GOLF BASKETBALL

Object: To practice basketball shooting skills.

Equipment: Several basketballs for each team.

Description:

Teams equal to the number of baskets are formed. A team goes to each basket where the instructor has marked eight different spots varying in range and position from the basket. Each player shoots until a basket is made at each spot. Players keep a record of the number of shots that they take before making the eight shots. The team whose players have taken the fewest shots is the winner.

SOCCEE

Object: To use soccer skills in a limited area.

Equipment: Ice hockey puck and goals.

Description:

The game is played with soccer rules except that a hockey puck is used, and it may only be kicked. The goalie may only kick the puck also.

BOTTLE LACROSSE

Object: To score goals by propelling the ball across the goal line using modified crosses.

Equipment: Small playground ball; a plastic bottle (with a handle and cut-off bottom) for each player; two goals; baseball glove for goalie.

Description:

Each team lines up on its half of the court with three forwards, two defensive players, and one goalie. The center forwards "dig" for the ball after it hits the floor on the referee's drop of the ball. The ball may be advanced by running with the ball cradled in the bottle or by passing the ball from the bottle to another teammate. Throws or catches made or assisted by a bare hand are penalized by the loss of possession. A point is scored when the ball is thrown from the bottle across the goal line. The goalie may catch the ball with the goalie's glove.

A score is followed by a drop ball. No boundary lines are necessary unless they are needed for safety. The penalty for illegally advancing the ball or catching the ball is loss of possession, with the opposing team awarded a free pass.

Variations:

1. Play outside and use more players.
2. Require the players to run sideways or use a designated form of locomotion.

INDOOR LACROSSE

Object: To throw a tennis ball into the basketball hoop while playing lacrosse rules.

Equipment: Lacrosse sticks; tennis ball.

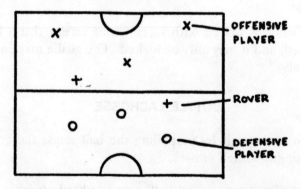

FIGURE 1-11. Player positions for Indoor Lacrosse

Description:

Each team is composed of eight players. There are three offensive, three defensive, and two rovers for each team. The offensive and defensive players must remain on their half of the basketball court and the rovers may play both offense and defense.

The game is played with lacrosse rules with each team attempting to throw the tennis ball through the basketball hoop.

Variation:

Use a heavier rubber ball to keep the ball from bouncing out of the cross. Use the backboard as a scoring area for less skilled players.

CIRCLE BOMBARDMENT

Object: To practice throwing skills.

Equipment: All sizes and shapes of balls.

Description:

Two teams are formed. Each team stays outside one-half of a circle drawn on the gym floor.

Each team throws balls at a ball placed in the center of the circle. The team that knocks the ball out of its opponent's half of the circle is the winner.

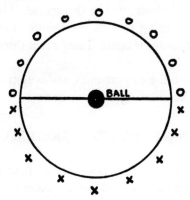

FIGURE 1-12. Team positions for Circle Bombardment

Variations:

1. Use different sizes and shapes of balls in the center of the circle to increase the difficulty.
2. Use a hockey puck or another flat object for skilled players.

CONE BOMBARDMENT

Object: To knock down the opponent's cone and win the game.

Equipment: Various balls; two cones.

Description:

A traffic cone is placed at each end of the floor. Vary the distance according to the ages and skills of the children. Players may take any position on their half of the court.

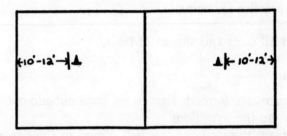

FIGURE 1-13. Cone placement for Cone Bombardment

The players throw the balls and attempt to knock over their opponent's cone and thereby win the game. The players cannot catch or hit a ball coming toward their cone, but they can throw another ball to protect their cone. They must throw from their own half of the court.

Teams are given the opportunity to develop strategy to protect their cone and strike their opponent's cone.

THREE-LEGGED BASKETBALL

Object: To teach students to coordinate their movements with those of classmates, and score baskets.

Equipment: One basketball and an elastic band for every two players.

Description:

There can be from six to ten players on a team. An elastic band is used to secure the inside ankles of two teammates. Basketball rules are played with some modifications. There are no backcourt violations and no time limit for bringing the ball across the mid-court line. The players tied together may pass (not hand) the ball back and forth to each other. Players must be in the front court before passing to other teammates in the front court. The ball is taken out at the location of an infraction and the ball need not be passed into play. Players are allowed two steps to begin a dribble and two steps to terminate a dribble.

JOGGING CIRCLE TOSS

Object: To earn points by tossing yarn balls in different sized circles while jogging.

Equipment: Two yarn balls for every member of one team; tire; hula hoop; rope.

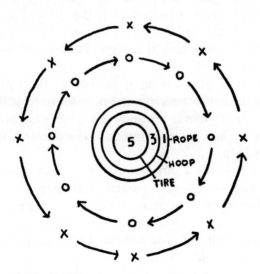

FIGURE 1-14. Team positions and directions of movement for Jogging Circle Toss

Description:

The tire, hula hoop, and rope are placed on the floor as shown. The team with the yarn balls forms a large circle and starts jogging counterclockwise. The other team forms a circle between the first team and the equipment and jogs clockwise holding arms high in the air.

Each player on Team One tries to toss yarn balls over Team Two into one of the center circles. One point is received for landing inside the hula hoop and five points for landing inside the tire. When all the yarn balls are tossed, the points are totaled and the teams change places. The team with the most points wins.

DOCTOR GOOD

Object: To finish the game with the fewest "wounded" players.

Equipment: Four pinnies to designate the doctors; eight to twenty yarn balls.

Description:

There are two teams and each team stays in its own half of the playing area. Two members of each team are doctors who can heal wounded players and get them back in the game. Each team starts with half of the yarn balls and attempts to hit the opponents. If a player is hit with a yarn ball, that player is wounded and must go to the pick-up area.

Doctors may drag wounded players by their feet from the pick-up area to their team's endline in order to treat the wounded players and permit them to return to the game. Players must protect their doctors so they are not wounded. If a doctor is wounded, no one else can help.

If a player holds a yarn ball for more than three seconds, it "blows up" and the player is wounded. Stepping over the center line also causes a player to become wounded. A player may catch a yarn ball without being wounded.

The team with the fewest number of wounded players at the end of the game is the winner.

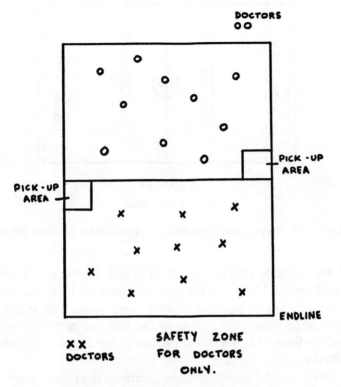

FIGURE 1-15. Playing area for Doctor Good

SCOOTER BOOM BALL

Object: To score goals by getting the ball to hit the wall after passing the goalies.

Equipment: A playground or soccer ball and a scooter for every two players.

Description:

Half of the players on each team are goalies who stand in the goal area and try to prevent the opposing team from hitting the wall behind them. The length of the wall up to a height of five to seven feet constitutes the goal area. The other half of the players on each

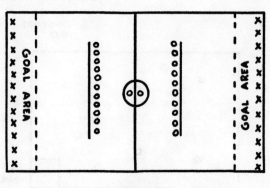

X – GOALIES
O – FORWARDS

FIGURE 1-16. Player positions and court set-up for Scooter Boom Ball

team are forwards who are on scooters and must stay between the two goal areas. The forwards can roll, pass, or kick the ball to a teammate to get in position to shoot for a goal. The forwards on defense attempt to gain control of the ball and move toward their end of the floor. When a goalie catches a shot or goal, the ball must be rolled out to a forward.

Goalies and forwards change positions after each point that is scored.

Variation:

Use two or three balls. Require the goalies to remain stationary.

CRAB SOCCER

Object: To score goals while crab walking.

Equipment: Soccer ball and goals.

Description:

This game is played on the gym floor with a goal at each end of the court. The goalie plays from a kneeling position and is the only person permitted to touch the ball with hands. The other players walk on their hands and feet, and may use any part of their body to block or advance the ball into the goal, except their hands. The game is started as in regular soccer.

TRASH CAN SOFTBALL

Object: To have an indoor game that will teach the fundamentals of softball.

Equipment: Four rubber bases; trash can; softball bat; six-inch playground ball.

Description:

Bases are placed in the usual softball position. The batting team gets four outs and then the teams change positions. Regular softball rules are used, except for the following modifications. The batter is out if:

1. the ball hits any part of the ceiling or light fixtures;
2. one strike (foul or swinging miss) occurs;
3. the ball is caught in the air even if it rebounds off a wall or bleacher; or
4. the bat is not placed in the trash can before running to first base. The trash can is placed near the first baseline approximately ten feet from home base.

SCOOTER-BALL HOCKEY

Object: To score a goal by putting the tennis ball in the goal.

Equipment: Scooter and table tennis paddle for each player; tennis ball; two goals.

Description:

Six players, including a goalie, are on each team. The players advance the tennis ball by batting, bouncing, or hitting it along the floor with a table tennis paddle. The ball may not be carried at any time.

Variations:

1. Have the players lie on the scooters.
2. Vary the striking implement and type of ball that is used.

SCOOTER ZONE BASKETBALL

Object: To score baskets from a sitting position on a scooter.

Equipment: Two standards with adjustable backboards or improvised baskets placed on the floor; one volleyball; scooters.

Description:

Each team has defensive players and offensive players who stay in their respective ends of the basketball court. The only way to move the ball is to pass it. The scooter cannot be moved when a player is in possession of the ball. The objective is to pass the ball from teammate to teammate to get in position for a good shot.

The basket should be no higher than five feet and may be a garbage can or similar container placed on the floor. Players are changed from offense to defense at the end of each period of play. Five-minute periods work out well.

Variations:

1. A specified number of passes can be required before taking a shot.
2. Only the nondominant hand can be used when passing.

MODIFIED STREET HOCKEY

Object: To develop street hockey skills and give every participant action.

Equipment: Four goal cones; six plastic hockey sticks and a puck for each game being played.

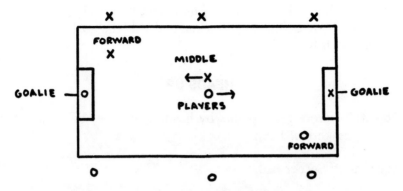

FIGURE 1-17. Player positions for Modified Street Hockey

Description:

Each team has six players with three players in action at a time, and three acting as sideline players who move up and down the sideline and kick the puck back onto the field of play. The players consist of a goalie, a middle player and a forward. The game is started with a face-off similar to field hockey. The teams play until one team scores. When a team scores, the forward player moves off the field and the first person in line moves into the goalie box, the goalie moves to become the middle player, and the middle player becomes the forward.

Variation:

Use timed periods and change the players at the end of each period.

CAGE BALL SCOOTER HOCKEY

Object: To kick the cage ball past the goalie.

Equipment: A cage ball and scooter for each player except the goalies.

Description:

The game is started at the center jump circle of the basketball court with the instructor throwing the ball above the heads of two players designated as captains. The object is to kick the ball past the goalie. The ball must be kicked and only the goalie can touch the ball with hands.

HEADS-UP

Object: To score team points by heading a soccer ball through a basketball hoop.

Equipment: Soccer ball.

Description:

The game is played on a basketball court with four to six players on a team and unlimited substitution permitted at any time. Hands can be used only after crossing the mid-court line when on offense. The dribble must "chip" the ball to a teammate so the ball can be caught. The ball is then thrown until it can be lobbed to a teammate to head at the basket. Scoring can occur only by heading the ball. Defense players can use their hands to try to intercept the ball that is being thrown. If the ball is intercepted, it must be dropped and dribbled past the mid-court line before it can be touched with the hands.

A coin flip determines who starts the ball. The game may be played in halves or quarters.

One point is scored for hitting the backboard, two points for hitting the rim, and five points for making a basket.

WALL SOCCER

Object: To develop soccer ball control skills and improve physical fitness.

Equipment: Soccer balls.

Description:

Two or four players can play. Rules are similar to one-wall handball, except that hands cannot be used. The serve must hit above the service line. After that, the entire wall is playable. The

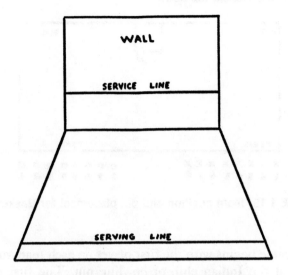

FIGURE 1-18. Wall Soccer playing court

ball may not bounce on the floor more than twice before being returned to the front wall. A game consists of twenty-one points, and a person or team can score only when serving. The size of the playing area should be determined by the age and skill level of the players.

Variations:

1. Play on an outside wall.
2. Increase the size of the playing area and add more players.

BASKETBOWL

Object: To score the most baskets after being the first to knock down a bowling pin.

Equipment: Two basketballs; two Indian clubs or bowling pins; one basketball goal for each game being played.

Description:

Two teams will compete against each other by setting up in the formation shown in Figure 1-19.

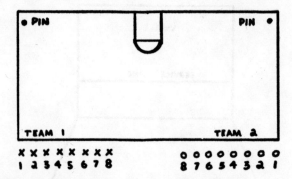

FIGURE 1-19. Team position and pin placement for Basketbowl

The game begins with the first player on each team rolling the basketball at the Indian club or bowling pin. The first player to knock down the pin will begin shooting baskets. The opposing player retrieves the other basketball and returns to make a chest pass to each member of the team (If both players miss the pin, they must run back to the starting line and bowl again.) After the chest passes are made, all players on that team must sit behind their team line. When this is done, the player on the opposing team stops shooting baskets. The number of baskets that the player made are counted and recorded. The game proceeds with each player having a chance to bowl and then either shoot baskets or pass to teammates. After a designated period of time, the team with the most baskets is the winner.

SCOOTER-SHOOTER

Object: To put the ball through the other team's goal.

Equipment: Twelve scooters; two goals; deflated soccer ball.

Description:

There are six players on a team and the players may move to any position on the floor. The ball is moved only by kicking. The game is played using two-minute shifts. Every two minutes another group of twelve players begins playing. No goalie may be used, and there is a free zone in front of each goal where scooters cannot enter. A dead ball in this area is given to the team defending that goal.

FIGURE 1-20. Goal area for Scooter-Shooter

Each two-minute period is started by dropping the ball between two opposing players in the center circle. The same procedure is used after a goal is scored.

Variations:

1. Have a goalie.
2. Permit the players to throw the ball but score only with a kick.

FIST BALL

Object: To return the ball before it bounces twice on the floor.

Equipment: Small cage ball; a net or rope.

Description:

A net or rope is placed at a height of three feet to divide a room or gymnasium. As many players as the space will accommodate may play. The game is started by using a bounce and underhand swing to serve. The ball is always hit with one or two fists. It may be hit against walls, the ceiling, or any other obstacles. A point is scored only on the serve, when the opposing team fails to return the ball before it bounces twice on their side of the net. The ball may be hit an unlimited number of times as long as it doesn't hit the floor twice. Spiking is not permitted.

Variation:

Use beach balls or volleyballs. Make it a cooperative game and see how many times the ball can pass over the net before it hits the floor.

BASKET-LONG BASE

Object: To score a run before the opposing team can make two foul shots.

Equipment: Basketball.

Description:

One team is in the field and one is at bat. The batter punches the ball that is lobbed to the plate and tries to run to the long base and back before the fielding team can take the basketball and pass it to a teammate who will make two foul shots.

There is a foul shooting order and batting order. If the batter scores before two foul shots are made, the batting team gets one point. If two foul shots are made before the batter scores, the fielding team receives a point. Every player bats and then the teams change positions.

Variations:

1. Change the number and type of basketball shots that must be made.

2. Play the game outside and require the fielding team to make a specified number of passes before the batter scores.

3. Provide other tasks for the fielding team.

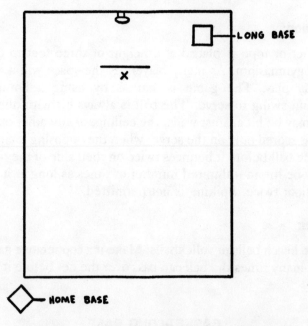

FIGURE 1-21. Basket-Long Base court diagram

CIRCUS

Object: To get around the bases before the outfielder makes a basket.

Equipment: Various sizes and types of balls such as ping pong, soccer, tennis, kickball, foam rubber ball, etc.

Description:

Divide the class into two teams. Each player is given a number corresponding to that of a numbered player on the opposing team. Three bases are set up in the gym and each team is assigned a basketball hoop at which it must shoot. The pitcher is given a box of various kinds of balls and may roll any one along the floor. When batter Number One kicks, any player may field the ball and pass it to fielder Number One who must make a basket before the runner gets around the bases. If the runner wins, her team gets one point. If the fielder wins, his team gets a point. Change sides after six players have been up to bat.

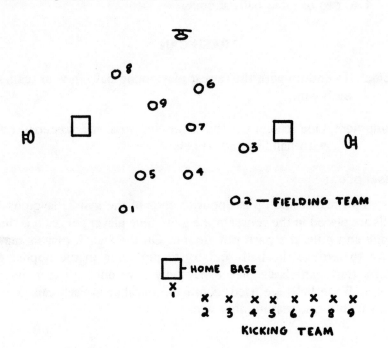

FIGURE 1-22. Court diagram and player positions for Circus

FREEBALL

Object: To be the last player to be free by avoiding the playground ball.

Equipment: One small playground ball or foam rubber ball.

Description:

One player starts with the ball. On the signal, the player tries to hit any other player below the waist with the ball. If the player is hit with a direct hit (not bouncing on the floor first, etc.), the player must squat down on the floor in that spot. That player may still receive the ball and hit others. If the ball is caught, neither the catcher nor the thrower has to squat down. The last person standing is the winner and starts the ball for the next round. The thrower may take only two steps with the ball and then must throw it.

Variation:

Use two or more balls at once.

TRASH CAN

Object: To end up with the fewest playground balls in your team's trash can.

Equipment: One scooter per child; two industrial size wastebaskets with handles and wheels.

Description:

Two teams line up at opposite ends of the gym. Playground balls are placed in the center of the gym. One player per team is the goalie and pulls the trash can around. On the signal, players may move to retrieve the balls and try to put them in the opposing team's trash can. Each player may only have one ball at a time. When all the balls are used, count the number in each can. The team with the lowest number wins.

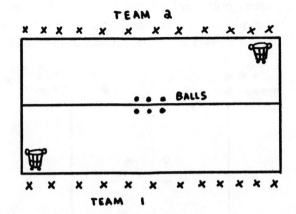

FIGURE 1-23. Court diagram and player positions for Trash Can

Additional Rules

1. Goalies must stay on their scooters at all times.

2. Goalies may bat balls out and move the trash can around, but may not tilt it or empty balls already inside.

3. All players must remain on the scooters and cannot touch trash cans, goalies, or other players.

4. Goalies may move anywhere on the floor.

PILLOW FIGHT

Object: To score points by landing "hits" with the pillow.

Equipment: Wrestling mat if indoors; grassy area if outdoors; four football helmets; four pillowcases with lightweight stuffing materials inside; four blindfolds.

Description:

Divide the class into four teams, each receiving a football helmet, blindfold, and "pillow." Start each team at a different corner of the square or mat. On the signal, the blindfolded player wearing the football helmet is directed toward the center of the square. When the player hits another on the head with the pillow, that player scores a point for his/her team. After thirty to forty-five seconds, change players. Team members may call out instructions to the blindfolded players but must remain in the corners.

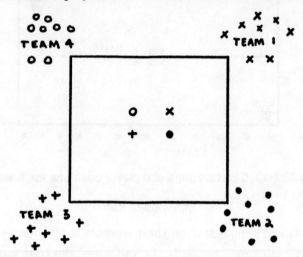

FIGURE 1-24. Court set-up and player positions for Pillow Fight.

2

Wait Until You Hear What We Did in Gym Today

42 New Twist Opportunities for Your Classes

Always look for new activities or new ways to use traditional games. This is what we emphasize in this chapter. Too often our minds set limits on the scope of activities in our physical education programs. We become accustomed to traditional activities and games and fail to capitalize on the potential of activities that are just being developed or those being used commercially. For example, in this chapter we include the slippery slide and roller skating activities. Both are used successfully in commercial recreational enterprises and can be used just as successfully in a physical education program. They provide the new twist that will keep your students returning eagerly to their physical education classes.

We hope that you will not only use the new twist activities that we have provided in this chapter, but that you will be receptive to ideas that will encourage you to come up with new twist activities of your own. Don't forget to use your students' ideas. Every ethnic group, every culture, and almost every community has games that are unique. Search out these games and incorporate them in your program. You will find that even traditional games contain different twists in different localities. Your students will be delighted if they are asked to share "their" games and "their" new twists.

To expand this idea, develop a joint project with a social science teacher and have your students write to children in other states and countries for descriptions of games and activities that are played in different localities and different cultures. You will be amazed at the ideas you will receive. This technique will also give your students the opportunity to teach new games, an element that increases the excitement of new twist activities in a class.

There are other good resources for new twist ideas. Scan columns and features in physical education and recreation journals devoted to new games and ideas. Share ideas with other innovative physical educators, especially at conventions and conferences, rich sources of ideas for your classes.

Children love to try activities that are different from what they commonly find in their physical education program. This is why new twist activities are so successful. The new challenge, the anticipation of trying a skill for the first time, a break from a usual routine, and the excitement heightened by the element of surprise, all contribute to the effectiveness of a new twist activity.

Keep in mind that new twist activities will meet your physical education objectives. These activities are oriented toward skill development and strengthening of motor abilities. Also, many are ideal for building physical fitness and reaching social and emotional goals. They should not be viewed as activities done simply to give your students a change or break from their regular program. New twist activities are fun, provide the variety that is important in maintaining enthusiasm, and, just as important, make it possible for you to attain the educational goals that you have for your classes.

Try the new twist opportunities in this chapter and you will be convinced!

FRISBEE

HULABEE

Object: To toss the frisbees so that they land completely inside the hula hoop.

Equipment: Five frisbees or coffee can lids and one hula hoop per group of five students.

Description:

Each player stands behind the restraining line and tosses one frisbee toward the hula hoop. One point is scored for each frisbee that lands completely inside the hoop. All players must remain behind the line until all of the frisbees have been thrown.

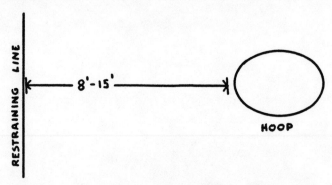

FIGURE 2-1. Hulabee playing area

Variations:

1. Score five points for each frisbee inside the hoop, three points for a leaner, and one point for each frisbee closest to the hoop. The first player to reach twenty-one points is the winner.

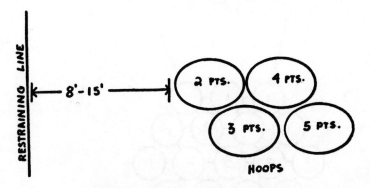

FIGURE 2-2. Variation of Hulabee court

2. Add more hula hoops and assign each hoop points according to the distance from the restraining line.

BULL'S-EYE FRISBEE

Object: To be the first player to reach twenty-one points by tossing the frisbee through the hoops.

Equipment: Ropes; mini-hoops or hula hoops; three frisbees; something from which to suspend the hoop target.

Description:

Tie the mini-hoops together so as to form an inner, middle, and outer circle. (Figure 2-3.) Suspend the entire "dart board" in the gym (from a basketball backboard, standard, or the like). The students start out at a distance of ten feet from the suspended hoops. Each player receives three throws from behind the restraining line. Three points are scored if the frisbee goes through the inner hoop, two points if it goes through the middle hoops, and one point if it goes through the outer hoops. The score is doubled if the player can name the circle of hoops (inner, outer, middle) through which the last of three throws will be thrown and is successful in the throw. At the end of the game, a player who has no chance of winning may elect to throw the last frisbee at the inner hoop. If successful, the game becomes an automatic tie and a play-off (three frisbee tosses per person) is played until a winner is determined.

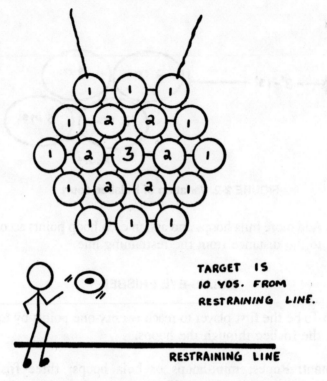

TARGET IS
10 YDS. FROM
RESTRAINING LINE.

RESTRAINING LINE

FIGURE 2-3. Bull's-Eye Frisbee Target set-up

Variation:

An individual may elect to throw at a moving target, in which case the hoops are swung and all point values are doubled.

FREE-FLY FRISBEE

Object: To be the first team to complete the designated task.

Equipment: Frisbee.

Description:

The class is divided into two teams. The team at bat throws the frisbee anywhere on the field. The batting team must then join together in some manner and move to a designated object (baseball backstop, hockey cage, bleachers, etc.) as quickly as possible. The fielding team, in the meantime, gets the frisbee and must have all of its players touch the frisbee. If the fielding team completes its task first, an out is scored against the batting team. If the batting team reaches base first, it scores a run. There are two outs per inning and the team with the most points after the designated number of innings, is the winner.

Variations:

1. The batting team must run in relay fashion to touch the base before the fielding team can throw the frisbee to each of its members.

2. Require each member of the fielding team to catch the frisbee. A player dropping the frisbee must catch another throw before the team's task is completed.

ALLEY-OOP

Object: To score a goal by sending a frisbee through a suspended hoop.

Equipment: Two hula hoops; one frisbee; string or rope.

Description:

Suspend a hula hoop from a basketball backboard or comparable standard. The distance from the ground may vary according to the age of the students and degree of difficulty desired.

Divide the players into two teams. The frisbee may be thrown, skimmed off the ground, or rolled to teammates. After three consecutive completed passes by a team, that team may try to score a goal by sending the frisbee through the hoop. If successful, a point is scored.

Each game is begun by flipping the frisbee to determine which team gets first possession at mid-court. The frisbee may be caught in the air, off a wall, on a roll, or when skimmed off the floor. If the frisbee is flat on the ground, it is not considered a completed

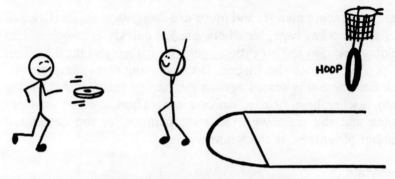

FIGURE 2-4. Hoop set-up for Alley-Oop

pass. If played indoors, use the three-second lane rule so that no player may set-up in front of the goal. If desired, designate a goalie's area.

Variations:

1. To increase the level of difficulty for a highly skilled group, allow only one-handed catches. Require that one or more throws be made with the nondominant hand.

2. Lower the hoops and play the entire game on scooters.

FRISBEE BLACKJACK

Object: To score twenty-one points by successfully catching the frisbee.

Equipment: One frisbee for each set of partners.

Description:

Players stand ten to fifteen yards apart and toss the frisbee back and forth. Throws must be accurate, within reach, and within five feet of each side of the receiver. One point is scored for a two-handed catch, three points for a catch behind the back, or between the legs. Twenty-one points is a game, and a player must win by two points.

Variations:

1. Gradually increase the distance between players and/or specify the type of throw to be used (forehand or backhand or a combination).
2. Have competition between partner teams. The objective would be to see which team could attain blackjack first.

SAUCER PONG

Object: To score points by causing the frisbee to land out of reach in the opponents' court.

Equipment: Tennis court; one frisbee for every four players.

Description:

Have four players set up on a tennis court as in tennis doubles. Keep score as in table tennis, alternating serves every five points. The frisbee is served, then tossed back and forth over the net. Only one serve is allowed per point. The frisbee must be returned from the spot at which it was received. Points are scored when a player fails to catch the frisbee or when it is thrown out of bounds.

Variation:

Play using tennis rules, regulations, and scoring.

SHIP TO SHORE FRISBEE

Object: To toss the frisbee and knock down the pin before the other teams can do the same.

Equipment: One frisbee per team; one pin or goal per team.

Description:

Divide the class into teams of no more than four. Each team member is given a number from one to four. On the signal, the first player tosses the frisbee towards the goal or pin. The second player runs to the frisbee and tosses from that point. Play continues until the pin is knocked down. When the pin falls, the entire team runs back to the starting line and sits in a single file. Points can be awarded for the first team to return to the starting point, and for the team knocking down the pin in the fewest tosses.

The football field is an ideal place for this activity.

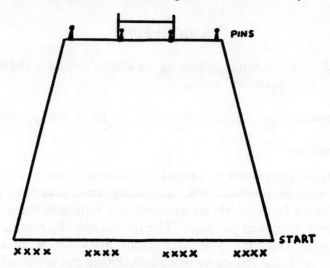

FIGURE 2-5. Ship to Shore Frisbee playing area

Variation:

Use two pins and place one pin at the starting point. The players must first knock down the far pin, then return and knock down the near pin before sitting in single file.

FROM KITE FLYING TO ROLLER SKATING

GO FLY A KITE

Object: To construct a kite that can fly successfully.

Equipment: Student designed preconstructed kites or store-bought kites; string.

Description:

This activity can be run in a variety of ways. One method is to announce a kite-flying contest for which students will provide their own materials and either construct kites at home or during class, perhaps in a science or art class. Small prizes could be awarded for the most cleverly designed kite, for the first kite to get in the air, the kite staying up the longest, etc. Physical activity will be provided as students run up and down the field trying to get the kite up. It has been found that students are easily motivated by this activity.

Variation:

If your budget permits, provide the materials so that all students or groups have identical materials, and challenge them to come up with the best flying design.

STILT-TILT

Object: To successfully complete the suggested challenges on stilts.

Equipment: Stilts constructed from metal or wood; store-bought stilts, or tin-can stilts; cones.

Description:

Some of the unusual activities described here can be used with other challenges mentioned in this chapter, and a station format can be used. Our suggestion is to place cards or posters listing the various challenges at each station for easy reference.

For younger children, construct tin-can stilts out of empty coffee cans and elastic. (See Figure 2-6).

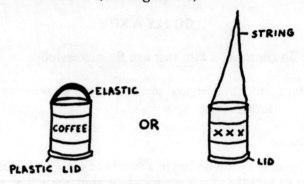

FIGURE 2-6. Tin-can stilts

Some sample challenges include:

1. Can you walk from A to B on the stilts?
2. Can you walk around the cone in a circle on stilts?
3. Can you zig-zag through the cones?
4. Can you walk over the shoe boxes?

The students who are waiting their turns should act as spotters and give helpful suggestions.

Variations:

1. To add an element of competition to this activity, have students keep track of their scores and times for each challenge. For example, see who can get from point A to point B the fastest or who can go around the cone the greatest number of times in one minute.
2. Teams can be set up and each individual's score computed for a team total.

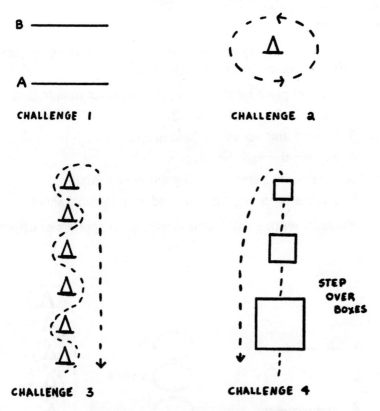

FIGURE 2-7. Sample Stilt-Tilt set-up

3. Allow students to invent their own games or challenges for others to try.

POGO-GO

Object: To successfully complete the suggested pogo stick challenges.

Equipment: One or more pogo sticks; beanbag; shoebox or small container; cones; hoops.

Description:

If you have access to a pogo stick, many challenging games and activities can evolve; challenges like:

1. Pogo in place for fifteen seconds without stopping.
2. Go from Point A to Point B.
3. Pogo in and out of the hula hoops.
4. Zig-zag through the cones.
5. How many times can you pogo in one minute?
6. Carry a bean bag with you and drop it into a shoebox.

Students waiting their turns should act as spotters or helpers.

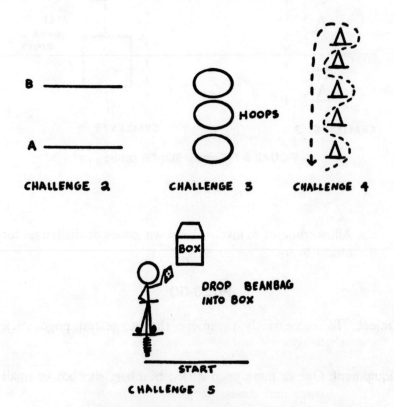

FIGURE 2-8. Sample Pogo-Go set-up

Variations:

1. Add competition by keeping times and scores for each challenge.
2. Allow students to invent their own challenges and games.

JUGGLE 'EM

Object: To successfully juggle one, two, or more tennis balls.

Equipment: Tennis balls (or softballs, yarn balls, beanbags, etc.).

Description:

Even though learning to juggle can be frustrating at times, it can increase eye-hand coordination and, once accomplished, can bring about strong feelings of success for students.

One Ball

1. Begin by having students toss one ball in the air and catch it in the same hand.
2. Toss one ball in the air and catch it in the opposite hand.
3. Toss the ball in the air, turn completely around, and catch the ball before it hits the ground.
4. Toss the ball over your shoulder and catch it behind your back before it hits the ground.

Two Balls

1. Toss both balls in the air at the same time and catch both.

FIGURE 2-9. Two-Hands Toss

2. Holding both tennis balls in one hand, toss one ball into the air. As it comes down, toss the other into the air and catch the first, etc.

FIGURE 2-10. One-Hand Toss

3. Holding one tennis ball in each hand, toss up one ball and transfer the other to the empty hand. Catch the first ball in the opposite hand.

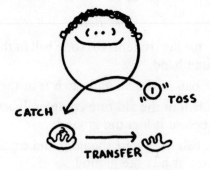

FIGURE 2-11. Transfer Toss

4. Holding one tennis ball in each hand, toss both in the air and catch each with the opposite hand.

FIGURE 2-12. Cross Toss

5. Holding one tennis ball in each hand, toss both into the air and do a full turn, trying to catch the balls before they hit the ground.

Three Balls

1. Hold two tennis balls in one hand and one in the other. Toss ball number one into the air and catch it in the opposite hand. As ball number one is descending, toss ball number two into the air and towards the opposite hand. As ball number two descends, toss number three and so on. When done correctly, the hands will move in an up and down pattern.

FIGURE 2-13. Three-Ball juggle

Variations:

1. Allow students to invent their own challenges for juggling one, two, three, or more balls.
2. Try partner juggling and have partners invent their own methods of juggling one, two, three, or more balls.

ROLLER SKATING CHALLENGE COURSE

Object: To teach safety rules and increase roller skating skills.

Equipment: Roller skates; cones; crepe paper streamers; hoops, trash cans; beanbags.

Description:

With the mounting popularity of outdoor roller skating, many students may own roller skates. If so, some unusual activities can be set up, and can provide an opportunity to review roller skating, skate boarding, and bicycling safety rules. A sample roller skating challenge course is described below:

Station 1: Cone Weave

Can you weave in and out of the cones forward? Backward? How many times can you weave in and out in one minute?

Station 2: Limbo

Have two students hold a crepe paper streamer at a height of four feet for the skater to go under. Gradually decrease the height and see who can go under at the lowest level.

Station 3: Beanbag Toss

Roller skate in a circle and try to toss beanbags into a trash can. Increase the distance from the trash can. Try going backwards.

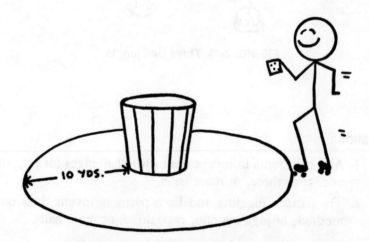

FIGURE 2-14. Set-up for Beanbag Toss

Station 4: Apart-Together

Set up cones as shown in Figure 2-15. Skate between the first set of cones with legs together, and then over the second cone with legs apart, and so on.

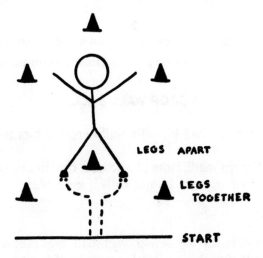

FIGURE 2-15. Cone placement for Apart-Together

Station 5: Forward-Backward

Skate forward to the first cone and smoothly switch to backward skating to the next cone, then switch to forward skating again, and so on.

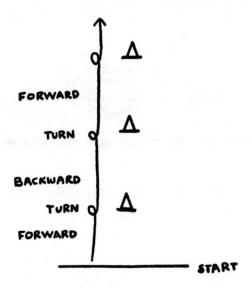

FIGURE 2-16. Cone placement for Forward-Backward

Variations:

1. Allow students to design their own stations and challenges.
2. Time stations or keep point totals for a competitive course.

SCOOP WALL BALL

Object: To catch the ball hit off a wall before it hits the ground.

Equipment: Scoops made from plastic milk containers; tennis balls; or lacrosse sticks and balls if available.

Description:

The boundaries for scoop wall ball are the same as for handball except that the court is lengthened if lacrosse equipment is used. Unlike handball, the ball must first hit the floor, and then the wall. The ball can be tossed with the hand, but the opponent must catch the ball in the scoop as it rebounds off the wall, and before it touches the floor a second time. If the ball is missed, the player who misses receives a point. The last to reach ten points is the winner.

In lacrosse versions, there is no checking and no interference. In either game, if a player blocks out or interferes with the opponent, he or she is given a point.

FIGURE 2-17. Scoop made from milk container

Variation:

Throw the ball by whipping it out of the scoop rather than throwing it with the hand.

GOLF ACTIVITIES

MINIATURE GOLF

Object: To complete the golf course using the fewest strokes.

Equipment: Hockey sticks; hockey, tennis, or golf balls; cones; hoops; flags and sticks; score cards; pencils; a chair; empty plastic bottles; boxes; tin coffee cans; ropes, pieces of rain gutters.

Description:

A golf course can be set up using any available equipment in your gym. Students may even wish to design their own miniature golf holes and try those designed by others. Samples for a nine-hole course could include:

Hole 1: Shoot the ball and hit the stick.

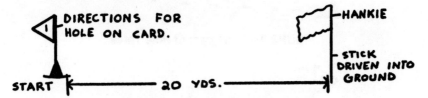

FIGURE 2-18. Diagram of Hole One

Hole 2. Shoot the ball into the empty shoebox, staying within the ropes. If the ball rolls out of the ropes, place it back in the ropes at the point it left and add a stroke penalty.

Hole 3. Hit the ball around the cone and into the tin can.

Hole 4: Hit the ball up the rain gutter and into the box.

Hole 5: Hit the ball around the cone and hit the suspended plastic milk carton (or bell).

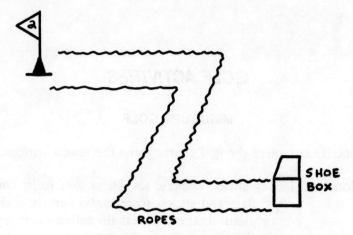

FIGURE 2-19. Diagram of Hole Two

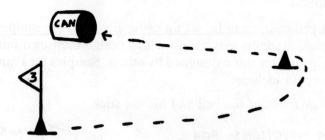

FIGURE 2-20. Diagram of Hole Three

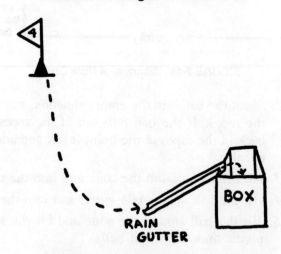

FIGURE 2-21. Diagram of Hole Four

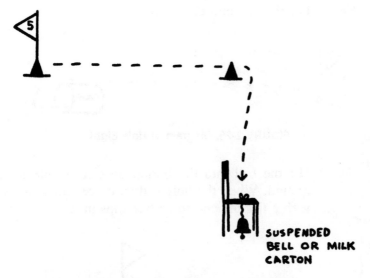

FIGURE 2-22. Diagram of Hole Five

Hole 6: Hit the ball through the maze and against the cone.

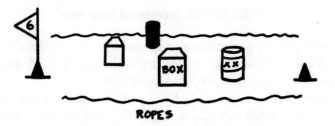

FIGURE 2-23. Diagram of Hole Six

Hole 7: Hit between the hoops and into the box. The ball must not enter the hoops or a one-stroke penalty is received. The ball is then placed back in bounds.

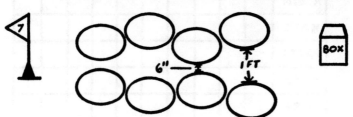

FIGURE 2-24. Diagram of Hole Seven

Hole 8: Hit the ball into the tin can.

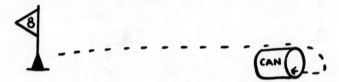

FIGURE 2-25. Diagram of Hole Eight

Hole 9: Hit the ball into the buried tin can or hole in the ground. When the hole is dug, be certain to mark it with a flag or cone so no one trips in it.

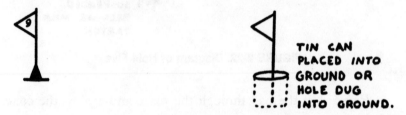

FIGURE 2-26. Diagram of Hole Nine

Any time a player has not gotten the ball to the designated spot in eight strokes, a two-point penalty is assessed, the player writes down a score of ten, and moves on.

Individual scores for the holes can be kept on a scorecard and groups of up to six can play at each hole, rotating when necessary.

GOLF COURSE CARD	1	2	3	4	5	6	7	8	9	TOTAL
ROBIN										
KATE										
PATTI										
BARB										
LORI										

FIGURE 2-27. Sample Scorecard

Variation:

For team competition, each group adds its respective scores, and the group with the lowest total wins.

FORE!

Object: To complete the modified golf course in the fewest strokes.

Equipment: Three-by-five cards; lime; nine cones; nine poles about five feet tall; nine marker flags (cardboard or folders). Staple the edge of the marker to the poles and place each pole in the center of marked circles. (See Figure 2-28.) Number each flag from 1-9. Also needed are 7-, 8-, or 9-iron golf clubs plus one or two golf balls per student.

Description:

Set up a golf course in the available space around your school. (Holes can be from 50 to 150 yards apart.) Mark each tee with a cone. For the "green," use a pole and mark two circles around it, one ten feet in diameter, and the other twenty feet in diameter. (See Figure 2-28.)

Divide the class into groups of up to four. Assign each group to different holes to start. (Shot Gun Start.) The groups then proceed in numerical order until all nine holes have been completed.

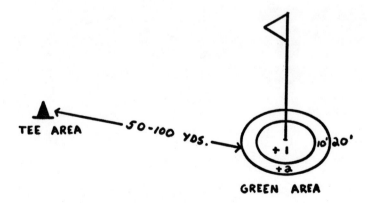

FIGURE 2-28. Diagram of playing area for Fore!

To keep score, count the number of times the ball is hit, starting at the cone for each hole, until the ball travels inside one of the marked circles. If the ball lands in the outer circle, the student picks up the ball and adds two strokes to his or her score for that hole. If the ball lands in the inner circle, the student picks up the ball and adds only one stroke to the total for that hole. A record of the scores should be kept on three-by-five cards provided by the instructor. A maximum of nine strokes is permitted per hole.

Variations:

1. Use plastic golf clubs and balls and shorter holes for younger children.
2. Add out-of-bounds areas and hazards such as goal areas or natural hazards (trees, bushes).
3. Use match play rules whereby the winner is the team that has won more holes than there are holes remaining to be played. Play single elimination or round robin match play. All types of golf competition can be played on a course of this type.

A SLIPPERY SLIDE
AND OTHER GREAT(??) IDEAS

SLIPPERY SLIDE

Object: To ride the slide as far as possible.

Equipment: Long piece of heavy-duty plastic (twenty-five or more yards); hose; grassy area (preferably a hill).

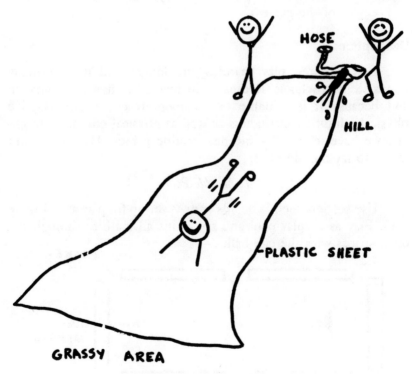

FIGURE 2-29. Slippery Slide layout

Description:

Lay the plastic on a grassy area and run water from a hose on the sheet to wet it. Leave the hose running at the top of the sheet of plastic. Students slide or carefully dive onto the sheet and slide as far as possible. (Be certain to have each student bring a towel and bathing suit, or tee shirt and shorts, the day of the activity.)

A contest can be run and awards can be given for the longest slide, fastest slide, or most original slide. Don't allow students to try the slide standing.

MARBLE MANIA

Object: To experience playing various marble games or invent new games.

Equipment: Marbles (equipment will vary depending on the design of the games).

Description:

Few children play marbles any longer and it is virtually nonexistent in schools. Because it increases eye-hand coordination and because it is valuable to classroom teachers and adaptive physical education instructors as well as physical education teachers, we have included some new marble games. However, don't forget to try the old ones.

1. Marble Pool

Use barriers such as boards or mats set-up for play as in Figure 9-30. Play as regular pool and try to hit all marbles through the open spaces with the cue ball.

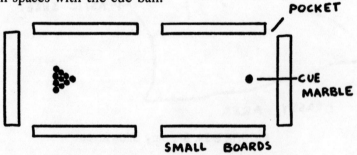

FIGURE 2-30. Playing area for Marble Pool

2. Marble Shuffleboard

This game is played as shuffleboard on a homemade wood court or on a taped gym floor or chalked playground surface. A backboard or wall is used for rebounding, and after each player has shot three marbles, collect them and start again.

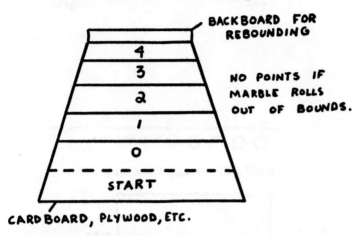

FIGURE 2-31. Diagram of Marble Shuffleboard playing area

3. Marble Golf

Have groups of students design various miniature golf holes using any type of material or equipment. Spools, paper towel tubes, cups, and other such items work well. Each group should write down the layout of the hole and the instructions for playing it. Have each group briefly explain the hole to the class and then allow the groups to try each other's inventions. Keep score as in miniature golf and save the design cards for future reference.

4. Marble Shooting Gallery

Set up a shooting gallery using objects of various sizes and shapes and assign a point value to each. Thread spools, paper cups, small boxes, or ping pong balls work especially well. Each student gets ten marbles to shoot while her partner keeps score. The player with the highest score, after each person has shot ten marbles, is the winner. Students can also design their own galleries.

5. Marble Croquet

Set up a croquet course using pipe cleaners taped to the floor. Regular croquet rules apply.

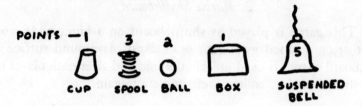

POINTS —1 3 2 1 5

CUP SPOOL BALL BOX SUSPENDED BELL

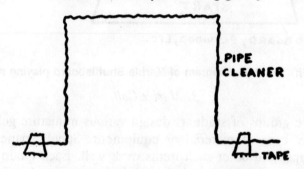

○ ○ ○ ○ ○ MARBLES

FIGURE 2-32. Sample shooting gallery

PIPE CLEANER

TAPE

FIGURE 2-33. Marble Croquet wicket

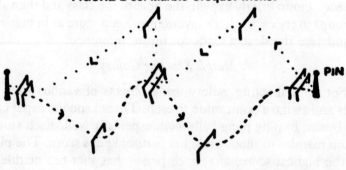

PIN

- - - → FORWARD COURSE

· · · · · → RETURN COURSE

FIGURE 2-34. Marble Croquet course

WIFFLE SCOOP BALL

Object: To score goals by tossing the wiffle ball into the trash cans.

Equipment: Scoops made from plastic milk cartons; wiffle balls; two large trash cans.

Description:

Two teams are spread out in the gym or on the field. The game begins with a center toss. Players pass the wiffle ball to each other using only the plastic scoops. After three consecutive passes, a team may attempt to score a goal by tossing the wiffle ball into the basket. No running or walking with the wiffle ball is permitted; only one step may be taken. If a pass is intercepted, the opposing team may go for a goal. Drawing a crease around the trash can which no player may cross adds more challenge to the game.

CREASE

FIGURE 2-35. Wiffle Scoop Ball playing area

Variation:

This game may also be played with a frisbee in place of the wiffle ball and scoops.

RAFTER BALL

Object: To send a tennis ball into the rafters causing it to land in a scoring zone on the gym floor.

Equipment: Tennis ball; floor tape.

Description:

Section half of a basketball court into eight-foot by eight-foot blocks, and mark each block with a 1,2,3, or 4. The one stands for a single, two for a double, three for a triple and four for a home run. Divide the group into two teams. The offensive team lines up off the court and the defensive team positions itself in and around the numbered blocks. The first offensive player throws the tennis ball into the rafters. As the ball finds its way onto the court, the defense tries to catch it before it hits the floor. If the ball is caught, the batter is out. If the ball is dropped, or if it hits the floor, the offensive player gets a base hit. The block in which the ball lands determines whether the hit is a single, double, triple, or home run.

Bases can be set up anywhere in the gym. Team scores can be computed on a sheet of paper or on a blackboard. A point is scored each time a runner crosses home plate.

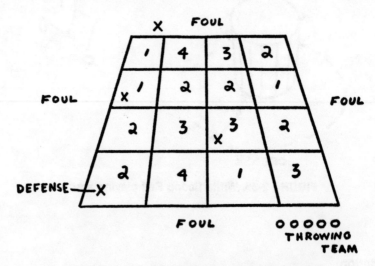

FIGURE 2-36. Court diagram for Rafter Ball

Each team receives three outs before changing from offense to defense. If a ball lands outside a marked area, it is a foul, and two fouls are an out. The offensive player may throw the ball from any point inbounds, but must throw it within five seconds from the time it is received. The winner is the person or team with the most runs at the end of a designated number of innings.

Variation:

Throw the ball toward the ceiling if your school does not have rafters or beams.

3

Two Left Feet— Not So Neat!

28 Ideas to Improve, or Start, Your Dance Unit

Many classroom teachers and even physical education teachers do not feel competent to teach dance. Yet, dance is a very natural extension of a comprehensive movement program and can be one of the most exciting units for students of all ages. Movement activities can lead smoothly into more formalized dances. After all, dance is movement in its purest form. Too often we get hung up on exact steps and style. We have found that students have no difficulty participating in structured dances provided they are able to move, are not embarrassed and can keep time to music. The activities in this chapter can be used by any teacher to provide a basic rhythm program that will prepare students to succeed in a more intensive dance unit in a physical education program.

As has been mentioned, many teachers do not feel comfortable teaching dance. However, the dance activities in this chapter do not require an extensive dance background. You can teach these activities and know that your students will enjoy the benefits of a rhythm program that is fun to do.

Young children will dance without inhibitions. Provide a setting for them to move and improvise as they enter into the dance activities in this chapter. Give them an idea or establish parameters in which they can move to music, and soon you will have a successful, fledgling dance unit.

Your older students can be a great help. Let them share their expertise by demonstrating the dances and other rhythms that are included in this chapter. In most classes you will have some students who have had some formal dance instruction. Use their knowledge and skill to increase the scope of your dance program. Use one or two of our dances and then let your students expand on them. Experienced dancers can share what they have learned, and the inexperienced dancers will be able to improvise by building on what they have learned in class.

Other great teaching aids are the tape recorder and record player. There are all kinds of records and tapes available not only to provide music, but also to explain the dance and lead your class through the dance with verbal instructions. Use these audio aids to increase the scope of your dance offerings.

One of your biggest challenges will be to involve students without embarrassing them. The activities we have included in this chapter are designed to have the students dancing before they realize that they are dancing. Once they find that rhythms are enjoyable, they will have overcome a major hurdle. They will also realize that they are capable of moving to music, and will be ready to enter wholeheartedly into a comprehensive dance program.

Too many boys have negative feelings about dancing. Part of the problem is lack of exposure as they are growing up. A ball is usually placed in their hands before they are able to walk. Naturally, they feel much more confident in a game where they are able to use the skills they have been developing for years. We have included dance activities that will utilize previously learned skills to minimize the strangeness that dance frequently has for the student who has not had exposure to this form of activity.

The activities in this chapter will stir student interest in dance and give your students the basic skills they need to participate fully in a dance program. You will also find the information you need to institute a dance unit if you have been one of the people who continually says, "I don't have the background to teach a dance unit."

BAG OF TRICKS

Object: To complete the movement problem in the designated tempo.

Equipment: Various tapes or records; two paper bags; task cards.

Description:

On one set of index cards, write various locomotor movements such as walk, hop, jump, run, leap, bend, twist, and gallop. Place these cards in one bag. On a second set of cards write various directional instructions such as forward, backward, sideways while turning, and upward, and place them in the other bag. Each student picks a card from each bag and must perform his task in time to the music. For example, if a student chooses cards that say "hop in a circle," then she must hop in a circle in time to the music.

FIGURE 3-1.

Variations:

1. Have the students perform one at a time, and have the class try to guess what the movement and direction are.
2. Have partners exchange cards and try to complete each other's tasks in addition to their own tasks.

MY TURN

Object: To have elementary students move body parts in time to the music.

Equipment: Records or tapes, number tags; tape.

Description:

Each member of the class is given a numbered tag to wear. In numerical order, starting with number one, each student will demonstrate moving a body part to the rhythm of the music. After everyone has had one turn, members of the class will go again, this time moving any two body parts. This procedure may continue until your students are moving several body parts simultaneously.

Variation:

Change the tempo of the music.

ZOO REVIEW

Object: To have students solve movement problems rhythmically.

Equipment: Records or tapes.

Description:

Set the tone by narrating an imaginary trip to the zoo. Throughout the game, stop the story and say, for example, "Let's visit the kangaroos! Show me how they travel." At this point, put on a record that has a bouncy, quick beat conducive to hopping. Continue the game as described, using music as often as possible. The "Baby Elephant Walk," "Popcorn" and "Pink Panther" are good songs for children to imitate.

Variations:

1. Assign each student an animal and have each imitate that animal's movement when it is mentioned in a story.
2. For extra credit, students could bring in records depicting certain animals.

MERRY-GO-ROUND

Object: To emphasize time, rhythm, space, and movement to younger students.

Equipment: Records or tapes; parachute; hula hoops.

Description:

As a beginning activity for young students, have them hold on to a parachute and walk in a circle while listening to a marching song or merry-go-round music. The children change direction on command and change their locomotor activity on command while keeping time to the music.

Next, play a song with four beats to a measure, preferably a popular tune that the children will recognize. Have the students count the beats aloud. After they have mastered this, have them perform a different activity to each beat. For example, clap the first beat and snap your fingers on two, three, and four, or walk on the first beat, jump on two, and hop on three and four. The possibilities are endless.

For another activity, have the children move the hula hoop to music or place the hoops on the floor and hop in and out on varying beats. Again, the possibilities are unlimited.

Variation:

Allow the students to determine the movements they will use, and have the entire class perform the movements that were suggested.

ME AND MY SHADOW

Object: To move your shadow in rhythm, performing the movement that the music suggests.

Equipment: Records or tapes; overhead projector.

Description:

This activity is similar to the overhead projector section, with another element added—rhythm. Place the overhead projector in a position so that students' shadows are cast on the wall. After an explanation of rhythm, begin by clapping your hands in a steady beat and ask your students to move their shadows in time to your clapping.

Play various types of music and have individual students or groups of students move in time, and have their shadows suggest the theme of the music. Some types of music include "76 Trombones," "Theme from Jaws," music from "Close Encounters" or "Star Wars," themes from TV shows, disco music, ballet, or classical music like the *1812* Overture, or the music from Muppet movies.

Variation:

Have groups of students perform to an entire song and demonstrate it to the class.

DISCO DRIBBLE

Object: To dribble a ball in time to the music.

Equipment: Records or tapes; one ball per student.

Description:

Music can be used effectively to teach a skill such as dribbling. Using a record with a slow tempo, have students dribble

FIGURE 3-2.

their balls in place to the music. As their skills improve, change to quicker and quicker tempos. To add an even further challenge, have them move in a designated pattern while still dribbling in time to the music. This activity also can be adapted to passing skills such as the chest pass and the bounce pass.

WHAT'S NEW?

Object: To have groups of students teach the class dance steps they have seen before or made up themselves.

Equipment: Popular records or tapes.

Description:

Divide the class into groups or partners and allow each to pick its own popular record. Have them put together a one- to two-minute sequence of dance steps to teach the class. The steps can be simple or complex, and they can be steps to popular line dances or steps the students have designed themselves. Choose the best group and have the group teach the dance to the class or to other groups. Also, if you are willing to learn, the students will usually be more willing to participate.

SAME DANCE, NEW TUNE

Object: To use well-known dance steps and perform them to popular music.

Equipment: Popular records or tapes.

Description:

Teach the steps to the "Alley Cat," "Bunny Hop" or a similar novelty dance. After the students have mastered the steps, play popular music and have them dance to that music. This generally is much more popular when the students recognize the music.

Variation:

Changing the speed of the music is often challenging and fun as the students try to keep up with the quicker beats. Be certain to do this after the students have mastered the steps, to avoid frustration.

FIGURE 3-3.

GYM JAM

Object: To perform dances or routines within a designated theme.

Equipment: Records or tapes.

Description:

While many schools hold gym shows, others may not have the budget to do so. We have found that choosing a theme and incorporating dances fitting that theme offers an interesting alternative. Groups of students may work together to develop steps or rhythmic activities for a holiday or season, or for themes such as hillbillies, outer space, circus, cowboys, TV shows, movies, etc.

Groups can compete for prizes or extra-credit points, with a panel of teachers for judges. Costumes can be improvised from simple materials. Allowing the students the freedom to choose the theme adds to their enthusiasm.

DANCE FEVER

Object: To teach students a wide variety of dances while allowing them to express their own creativity.

Equipment: Records or tapes.

Description:

A unit in dance can take on new excitement if each day or lesson offers variety. Students who are average square dancers may find themselves excellent social dancers. A dance program can be broken down into categories such as social, square, folk, fifties, disco, and jazz and the students could be asked to perform one dance from each category. Each day a new dance could be taught: the Cha Cha on Monday, the Hustle on Tuesday, and a square dance on Wednesday.

Some dances that can be included are:

Social	Square	Folk	Fifties	Disco
Cha Cha	Virginia Reel	Irish Jig	Sloopy	Latin Hustle
Waltz	Red River Valley	Tarantella	Mash Potatoes	Camel
Charleston		Polka	Swim	Bus Stop
Rumba			Monkey	4-Step
Fox Trot			Jitterbug	
Alley Cat			Pony	
Bunny Hop			Twist	
Limbo				

Variation:

As a culminating activity, have students attend a hop or hoedown and have them dress up appropriately.

FIGURE 3-4.

COUNTDOWN

Object: To perform various movements in their correct sequence and in time to the established beat.

Equipment: None.

Description:

Divide the class into circles of four to six students. Give each student a number. The instructor begins by performing a movement such as a clap. Student Number One then claps and adds a movement of his own such as slapping the floor; student Number Two claps, slaps the floor and adds another movement. This continues around the circle. The movements should be done in time (such as ¼ time) and any student who breaks the rhythm or misses the sequence is given a letter "C" in countdown. Another letter of the word COUNTDOWN is given each time the rhythm or sequence is missed. The last student left is the winner. This game should be used only after students are no longer self-conscious about dancing.

SOLDIERS

Object: To follow commands and remain in time to the music.

Equipment: March records or tapes.

Description:

Marching can be an effective and entertaining way to teach tempo, rhythm, etc. Using either single line or column formations,

FIGURE 3-5.

the students follow the instructor's commands. Marching music is played and students must remain in time to the beat. Commands may include attention, left face, mark time, forward march, backward march, to the rear march, sideward march, halt, and to the left and right oblique.

Variations:

1. Allow students to take turns as commander.
2. Speed up the tempo of the music used.
3. Have squads compete.

EIGHT COUNT

Object: To solve the designated movement problems correctly.

Equipment: Drum for instructor.

Description:

The class is given various movement challenges that it is to complete in eight counts. (As the class progresses, twelve, sixteen, or more counts can be used.) This activity works best with partners, one partner observing or helping the other. The instructor beats eight counts on the drum while the students perform for their partners. The observing partner then gets to perform. Some sample problems are:

1. Walk forward on counts 1-2-3 and 4. Hop on 5 and jump on 6-7-8.

2. Walk backward on counts 1-2-3 and 4, hop backward on 5 and jump backward on 6-7-8.

3. Leap 1, run 2-3-4, hop 6-7-8.

4. Walk 1-2-3-4, turn 6-7-8.

5. Walk low-1, high-2, low-3, high-4, jump low-5, jump high-6, jump low-7, jump high-8.

The variations and combinations are endless. Students also may wish to design their own problems for others to try.

Variations:

1. Using music rather than a drum beat, perform eight-count gymnastics and tumbling exercises. (Example: cartwheel-2-3-4, hitchkick-6-7-8.)

2. For advanced classes, partners not only can duplicate the eight-count patterns, but they can also try to reverse them for an added challenge.

4

No Johnny, You May Not
Use Your Math Book
for Home Plate!

99 + Activities
for the Classroom

Both the classroom teacher and the physical educator who teaches some classes in a classroom will find this chapter valuable. Even if the children have another physical education period during the day, the classroom teacher can use the activities to provide a lift for the children or to give them a change of pace if they become restless after prolonged sitting at their desks, or to supplement the regular physical education program. Too often, schools do not have daily physical education classes. The ideas in this chapter can be used by the classroom teacher to provide physical education activities on days when they are not scheduled for physical education. The activities are also excellent as recess activities on days when the children cannot go outside. Students will still get their physical activity and the variety of activities will keep the students stimulated even in a relatively small space. These activities should also be considered for use during activity periods if your school is structured to include time for different student activities.

Most elementary school physical education teachers will at some time or other teach physical education in a classroom, either because of inadequate facilities or because the gymnasium is being used for another purpose.

This chapter can be used to develop a classroom unit. The physical educator also should consider scheduling a physical education class or even a short unit for the classroom periodically. Having physical education in the classroom will generate excitement if it is done infrequently. Even more important, it helps to make the children aware that physical education is just like their other subjects. It becomes easier for the children to understand that physical education is an integral part of the curriculum.

Physical education teachers may want to use some of these activities in the gymnasium also. Many of them are excellent for use in a station format. They are also ideally suited for use on days when only a portion of the gymnasium is available.

This chapter contains several different kinds of activities. There are team and group games. Plenty of movement and group efforts are provided even though the games are designed for the limited space that is found in the classroom. Individual pupil activities are uniquely developed for individual fitness and skill development. Too often we don't think fitness development is possible in a classroom. This chapter shows you that it can be done! Motor development and fine motor skills also result from participating in these activities.

What's more, it is important for teachers to correlate the learning materials and experiences of different subjects. One section of this chapter shows different ways that physical education can be correlated with other subjects; this is important if physical education is going to make a maximum contribution to each child's education. Both the classroom teacher and the physical education teacher can use these activities to strengthen what the students are studying in other areas. We strongly support the principle of all teachers working closely to provide the best possible educational experience for every student. Activities that correlate what is happening in the gymnasium with what is happening in the classroom provide an opportunity to work toward this goal.

The activities in this chapter will add a valuable dimension to your classroom physical education program.

TEAM AND GROUP ACTIVITIES

ELECTRICITY

Object: To stimulate enthusiasm during a physical education class.

Equipment: None.

Description:

This game can be played sitting at desks in rows, or standing in the aisles. The players grasp one hand of the person in front of them, and one hand of the person behind them. The first person in each row is the leader. When the teacher shouts "electricity," the leaders squeeze the hand of the person behind them and this flow of electricity is sent to the back of the line. The last person sends the electricity forward. When the electricity returns to the front of the line, the leader raises her hand to signify that the electricity has made a complete circuit. The first team with a complete circuit wins the contest.

Variations:

1. Have each team do a movement activity or perform a physical skill when it has a completed circuit. Examples would be running in place while counting to 100 if standing, or tossing a foam rubber ball from one hand to the other 50 times if sitting. When every member of a team has completed the task, another circuit is formed and the team completing this circuit wins the contest.
2. Teams can also use a circle formation if space permits.

YARN BALL VOLLEYBALL

Object: To learn the rules of volleyball and develop catching and throwing skills.

Equipment: Yarn ball and string or rope.

Description:

Chairs are placed facing each other in an equal number of rows. A rope or piece of string is stretched across the room to serve as a net.

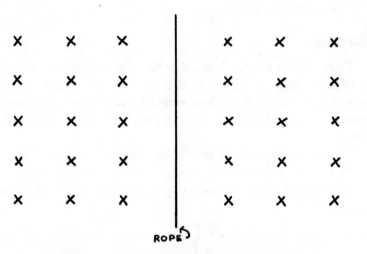

ROPE

FIGURE 4-1. Playing area for Yarn Ball Volleyball

A yarn ball is used as a volleyball. Out-of-bounds is the area just beyond the reach of those players at the end of each row and behind those in the back row. The yarn ball is passed over the net. If it is caught, it must be passed to three different players before it can be returned over the net. Games are scored as in volleyball. Players may not get out of their chairs while the ball is in play.

Variations:

1. Have the players rotate positions as in volleyball.
2. Require students to use only one hand and then only the nondominant hand as their skills increase.
3. Place a sheet or similar covering over the rope to block the receiving team's view.

MUFFIN BAKE

Object: To blow a table tennis ball into a muffin tin.

Equipment: One muffin tin (twelve-muffin size); four pieces of cardboard to make a ramp for each side of the muffin tin; six table tennis balls (three of one color and three of another).

Description:

Draw a circle on the floor about five feet in diameter. (Vary the size of the circle according to the ages of your students.) The players lie on the floor on their stomachs with their chins outside the circle. The muffin tin and ramps are placed in the center of the circle.

The table tennis balls are placed randomly around the circle. The players, who have been divided into two teams, try to blow their table tennis balls up the ramps and into the tin. The game

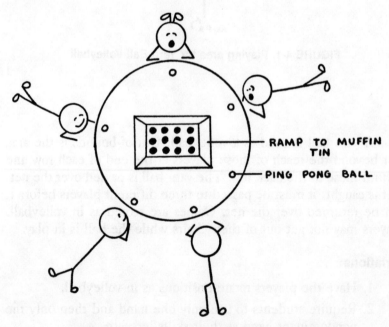

FIGURE 4-2. Positions for playing Muffin Bake

should be played with one- or two-minute rounds. If space is limited, new teams can be substituted at the end of each round.

Variations:

1. Increase the number of table tennis balls that are used.
2. Use the top of a table or push several desks together if it is not possible to play the game on the floor.
3. Give different values to different colored tennis balls.

TIC-TAC-TOE

Object: To be the first team to align three players in a straight line.

Equipment: Foam rubber basketball; wastebasket; a tic-tac-toe diagram drawn on the floor for each team.

Description:

Two teams line up facing the wastebasket which has been placed ten to twenty feet away. The teams alternate trying to shoot the ball into the basket. A successful attempt allows the player to take a seat within the tic-tac-toe diagram.

A player who misses goes to the rear of his team's line to wait his next turn. Teams try to get three players in a straight line. They also use strategy to block their opponents.

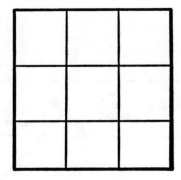

FIGURE 4-3. Tic-Tac-Toe diagram

Variations:

1. Use beanbags instead of foam rubber basketballs.
2. Use math problems or questions from some other subject to determine who gets to sit on the tic-tac-toe board.
3. Require a specific locomotor movement to go to the tic-tac-toe board.

SWEEP-UP DERBY

Object: To score the most points by knocking down more pins than the opposing team.

Equipment: Seven plastic bowling pins (or empty plastic household bottles); four cones; one frisbee; one push broom.

Description:

Each player stands behind the foul line when shooting. The first player takes the broom and places the frisbee on the ground in

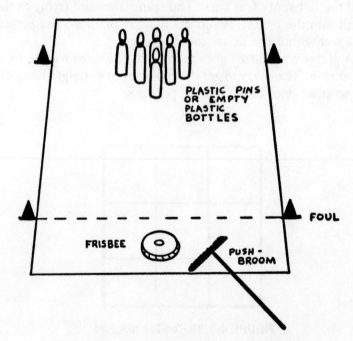

FIGURE 4-4. Sweep-Up Derby court diagram

front of it. The player pushes the frisbee towards the pins in an attempt to knock down all the pins. Each player has two consecutive attempts. If the foul line was crossed while shooting, the player's score for that turn does not count. One point is scored for each pin down with a two-point bonus for a strike and a one-point bonus for a spare. To keep the game relatively simple, add frame scores together rather than use official bowling scorekeeping. Either a time-limit or point-limit game can be played.

FLEXIBILITY PROGRAM

Object: To teach students flexibility exercises and proper stretching techniques.

Equipment: None.

Description:

Distribute your students around the room so they have their own spaces. Describe proper stretching techniques and then have your students do partner and individual stretching. Provide flexibility exercises for the various body parts so that each student will have a personal flexibility program.

The flexibility program can be used as an initial warm-up routine for each class period after your students become familiar with the techniques you have taught them.

ADDITIONAL GAMES AND ACTIVITIES

There are many other team and group activities in other chapters that are ideal for use in the classroom. Some of them need to be modified or changed slightly in order to fit into the space provided by a classroom.

We suggest you consider the following activities:

Chapter 2 – Hula Bee, Go Fly a Kite, Stilt-Tilt, Juggle 'Em, Marble Mania

Chapter 3 – Bag of Tricks, My Turn, Zoo Review, What's New?, Same Dance, New Tune, Count Down

Chapter 5 – Several appropriate ideas

Many activities in our first book are also perfect for use in the classroom.* Examine the following activities to expand your classroom excitement:

There are additional activities in this book that could also be used in the classroom. Make changes that are required or simply use a game idea and develop your own modification to fit your space and students' interests.

*Kenneth G. Tillman and Patricia Rizzo Toner. *What Are We Doing in Gym Today?* (West Nyack, NY: Parker Publishing Co., Inc., 1983)

INDIVIDUAL PUPIL ACTIVITIES
FOR FITNESS AND
SKILL DEVELOPMENT

The activities in this section were developed by Mr. Charles "Chick" Cosover, an elementary physical education teacher in Teaneck, New Jersey. For these activities, the classroom is organized with up to thirty-five stations distributed throughout the class. The stations can be arranged according to environment and the workable spaces within each of them. The number of activities selected for each class period should be the same as the number of students in the classroom. All of the activities are performed for one minute, and then scores are recorded by the students on a self-testing scorecard. (A sample scorecard is presented at the end of this section.) Then they move to the next station. Students are encouraged to do as well as possible at each station. They do not compete against other students but against themselves in an attempt to improve their own performance each time the activity stations are used during a physical education period. You will find that many of your students will be motivated to practice these activities on the playground and at home.

CATCH A BALL

Object: To develop proficiency in catching skills and improve eye-hand coordination.

Equipment: A piece of newspaper and masking tape, or a tennis ball.

Description:

Make a ball from a piece of newspaper wrapped with masking tape, or use a tennis ball. Throw it into the air and catch it. Do this continuously, making as few errors as possible in one minute.

Encourage the pupils to catch the ball in their hands rather than trapping it between the arms and chest.

Self-Evaluation:

Count and record the number of errors made in one minute.

Variations:

1. Specify that the ball must be tossed above head height each time.
2. Use one hand or nondominant hand.
3. Throw with one hand and catch with the other.

THROUGH THE STICK

Object: To improve flexibility.

Equipment: Wand or yardstick, or any two- to three-foot stick.

Description:

Pupils stand holding a wand or stick in both hands behind their backs. They bring the wand up over their heads and in front of their bodies without releasing either hand. Then, they step over the wand with one foot and then the other until they have returned to their original positions. Remind the children that the wand must always be held with both hands.

Self-Evaluation:

Pupils count and record the number of times they complete this task in one minute.

WALK A ROPE

Object: To improve balance.

Equipment: A piece of rope approximately six feet long.

Description:

The student walks the length of the rope alternately putting one foot in front of the other with the feet always pointing straight ahead. After reaching the end of the rope, the student turns on the rope and repeats the task. Keeping the arms outstretched is often helpful in maintaining balance.

Self-Evaluation:

Pupils count and record the number of times that one foot is not in contact with the rope during the one-minute period.

RUN IN PLACE

Object: To improve cardiovascular fitness.

Equipment: None.

Description:

Run in place. Feet should always be lifted from the floor.

Self-Evaluation:

Pupils count and record the number of times they must stop to rest during the one-minute period. Older children may want to count the number of times one foot touches the floor.

BEANBAG TOSS

Object: To improve target tossing skill.

Equipment: Twelve beanbags and a wastebasket.

Description:

Standing ten feet from a wastebasket, the student attempts to toss the beanbags, one at a time, into the basket. When no beanbags remain, the student runs to the basket, retrieves the beanbags and returns quickly to the starting point where the tossing continues. Encourage pupils to explore different ways of tossing the beanbags.

Self-Evaluation:

Pupils count and record the number of beanbags they get into the basket.

Variation:

Specify different ways that the beanbag is to be thrown.

JUMPING OVER ROPE

Object: To improve cardiovascular fitness and improve eye-foot coordination.

Equipment: Jump rope or a piece of rope six to eight feet long.

Description:

The student jumps (or hops) continuously on alternate sides of a rope which is placed in a straight line on the floor. The student moves sideways, or from front to back, without touching the rope.

Self-Evaluation:

Students count and record the number of times they touch the rope in one minute. Older students count the number of times they cross the rope.

SIT-UPS

Object: To strengthen abdominal muscles.

Equipment: None.

Description:

Students lie on their backs, knees bent, feet flat on the floor. They clasp their hands behind their necks. They raise their torsos to a sitting position and touch elbows to knees. They lie down slowly and repeat the procedure.

Self-Evaluation:

Students count and record the number of sit-ups they complete in one minute.

BALLOON SOCCER

Object: To improve eye-foot coordination.

Equipment: Balloon.

Description:

Students hold a balloon at waist height, drop it to their feet and attempt to keep it in the air for as long as possible using only feet and legs.

Self-Evaluation:

Pupils count and record the number of times the balloon touches the floor.

DRIBBLING A BALL

Object: To improve a popular ball handling skill and improve eye-hand coordination.

Equipment: Six-inch or eight-inch playground ball, or basketball.

Description:

Students attempt to dribble a ball with one hand for as long as possible. If the ball gets away, they regain possession and start again. Pupils should be taught that the fingers, not the palm of the hand, exert the force on the ball, pushing it to the floor. Knees should be bent slightly.

Self-Evaluation:

Pupils count and record the number of times they lose possession of the ball.

STANDING LONG JUMP

Object: To develop leg power.

Equipment: Masking tape (if needed).

Description:

The pupil stands behind the starting line and jumps forward as far as possible, with both feet involved simultaneously at take-off and landing. Measure the jumping distance by placing masking tape at various intervals on the floor. (If a floor has square tiles or other uniformly marked intervals, masking tape is not needed.) Practice and measure several jumps. Pupils should bend their knees before jumping, and thrust arms out during the take-off from the floor.

Self-Evaluation:

The pupil marks the distance of the jumps determined by the part of the body that touches the floor closest to the starting line. The best jump is recorded.

ONE-LEG BALANCE

Object: To improve balance.

Equipment: None.

Description:

The student stands on one leg. Hopping, pivoting, or moving the leg in any way is not permitted. Keeping arms outstretched will often be helpful in keeping balance.

Self-Evaluation:

Students count and record the number of errors made. An error involves loss of balance that causes the leg to pivot or lift from the floor.

HANG OVER DOOR

Object: To develop upper body strength.

Equipment: A chair and a door.

Safety Considerations:

1. The teacher must be certain that the door remains immobile at all times.
2. A sturdy chair for the pupils to stand on is placed alongside a door.
3. Children must be cautioned to step on and off the chair carefully.

Description:

Students place their hands on top of the door. They pull up from the chair so that their chins are above the door and their feet are not touching any surface. When tired, the students may lower themselves to the chair placed a few inches under the feet and then, after a brief rest, pull up again. Kicking is not permitted.

Self-Evaluation:

Pupils count and record the number of times they descend in one minute.

SHUTTLE RUN

Object: To improve agility and cardiovascular fitness.

Equipment: Two chalkboard erasers.

Description:

Two erasers are placed on the floor, approximately ten feet apart. By running back and forth, the pupil touches the erasers as often as possible in one minute. Do not move the erasers. The distance should remain the same.

Self-Evaluation:

Pupils count and record how many touches are made in one minute.

Variation:

Teachers may elect to have pupils move back and forth while sitting or kneeling on a scooter.

BUILDING CHECKERS

Object: To improve small muscle coordination.

Equipment: Forty-eight checkers or dominoes.

Description:

Build a vertical column of checkers using as many as possible.

Self-Evaluation:

Pupils count and record how many checkers are stacked in the column after one minute.

MAKING TENTS

Object: To improve small muscle coordination.

Equipment: A deck of playing cards.

Description:

Students take two cards and get them to stand in an upright position by leaning them on each other. They continue making as many tents as possible. Students should be cautioned not to build tents too close together to avoid knocking other tents down.

Self-Evaluation:

Students count and record the number of tents that remain standing after one minute.

BEANBAG CATCH

Object: To improve small muscle coordination.

Equipment: Beanbag.

Description:

The student throws a beanbag into the air, claps hands together once, and then attempts to catch the beanbag. If successful, the student again throws the beanbag up, claps twice, and attempts to catch the beanbag. After each success the pupil claps an additional time on each succeeding toss.

Self-Evaluation:

The students count and record the highest number of times they are able to clap their hands together before successfully catching the beanbag.

STEP-UPS

Object: To improve cardiovascular fitness and develop leg strength.

Equipment: Low, solid chair.

Description :

The pupil steps up onto a chair and down, one leg at a time. The body must remain upright at all times (using good posture.)

Self-Evaluation:

Pupils count and record the number of times they step down from the chair.

STANDING ON TIPTOES

Object: To improve balance and develop leg strength.

Equipment: None.

Description:

The pupil rises to tiptoe position, heels raised as far as possible from the floor, and holds this position for as long as possible. If forced to descend because of loss of balance or fatigue, the tiptoe position is assumed again as soon as possible.

Self-Evaluation:

Pupils count and record the number of times they are forced to descend from the tiptoe position.

"V"-SIT

Object: To develop abdominal and leg strength.

Equipment: None.

Description:

The pupil sits on the floor, legs together and straight, arms outstretched, to the sides, parallel to the floor. Legs are raised as high as possible, keeping them straight, maintaining balance on the buttocks without using hand support. If the student is forced to lower his legs because of loss of balance or fatigue, the legs are raised to this position again.

Self-Evaluation:

Pupils count and record the number of times they are forced to descend from the "V" sit position.

BICYCLE RIDE

Object: To strengthen abdominal and thigh muscles.

Equipment: None.

FIGURE 4-5. Body position for "V"-Sit

Description:

Pupils lie on their backs and raise their legs and lower trunks as nearly vertical as possible. The weight supporting the upper body is on the back of the shoulders and the hands are placed on the floor to provide balance. Pupils make bicycling movements with their legs.

Self-Evaluation:

Pupils count and record the number of times they are forced to stop and rest during one minute.

FORWARD BALANCE

Object: To improve balance and flexibility.

Equipment: None.

Description:

The pupil stands on one foot and bends forward, raising the free leg backward until both the trunk and free leg are parallel to the floor. Arms are held at right angles to the body. The position is held as long as possible.

Self-Evaluation:

Pupils count and record the number of times they are forced to descend from this position.

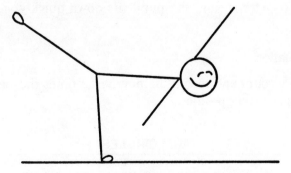

FIGURE 4-6. Body position for Forward Balance

WRITING BEHIND

Object: To improve flexibility of spine and leg muscles.

Equipment: Chalk.

Description:

Students stand bent forward, feet wide apart. They reach back through their legs as far as possible and make a mark on the floor with a piece of chalk (if chalk is not feasible, an object such as an eraser may be set down, but not thrown.) The goal is to make a more distant mark on each attempt.

Self-Evaluation:

Students measure and record the distances they are able to reach behind and through their legs using markings on the floor.

SIT TO STAND

Object: To improve agility

Equipment: None.

Description:

The pupil sits on the floor with arms folded in front of the chest. The objective is to rise to a standing position using only legs for support. After rising, the pupil sits down quickly and repeats this task.

Self-Evaluation:

Pupils count and record the number of times they are able to come to a standing position.

ARM CIRCLES

Object: To improve flexibility of the shoulder joints and develop strength of the shoulder muscles.

Equipment: None.

Description:

The pupil may sit or stand while making circular arm movements, keeping the arms straight. The pupil may alternate between forward and backward circular movements.

Self-Evaluation:

Pupils count and record the number of times they are forced to stop and rest.

PLAYING DICE

Object: To improve small muscle coordination.

Equipment: Pair of dice.

Description:

The pupil picks up and throws a pair of dice, first with one hand and then with the other. A point is scored each time a double (same number on both dice) is thrown. Although throwing a double is pure chance, pupils should be reminded that if they are quick and throw the dice often, their chances of throwing doubles are increased proportionately to the number of throws they make.

Self-Evaluation:

Pupils count and record the number of doubles they throw.

BEANBAG KICK

Object: To improve eye-foot coordination.

Equipment: Beanbag.

Description:

The pupil places a beanbag on the instep of one foot, kicks it up, and attempts to catch it.

Self-Evaluation:

Pupils count and record the number of successful catches they make.

CRAB CIRCLES

Object: To strengthen arm and abdominal muscles.

Equipment: Hula hoop.

Description:

The pupil assumes a crab position—the body is supported by the hands and feet, with the knees at right angles. The pupil crab walks around the outside of the hula hoop, moving either forward, backward, or sideways.

Self-Evaluation:

Pupils count and record the number of complete circles they make around the hula hoop.

HOOP DROPS

Object: To improve flexibility.

Equipment: Hula hoops.

Description:

Pupils stand, holding hula hoops over their heads. They lower the hoops around their bodies, step out of them, raise them over their heads again and repeat the task.

Self-Evaluation:

Pupils count and record the number of times they are able to lower the hoop around the waist.

FIGURE "8"

Object: To improve trunk flexibility and ball handling skills.

Equipment: Playground ball (six-inch or eight-inch diameter).

Description:

Students stand on the floor with their feet shoulder-width apart. They bend forward and roll a ball, guiding it carefully with the hands between and around their legs. The path of the ball makes the figure "8."

Self-Evaluation:

Pupils count and record the number of times they are able to make the figure "8."

SCOOP BALL

Object: To improve eye-hand coordination.

Equipment: Tennis ball; scoop (cut out the bottom of a plastic bleach container).

Description:

The pupil stands and faces a wall three feet away. The pupil throws the tennis ball against the wall with one hand and attempts to catch it in the scoop which is held in the other hand.

Self-Evaluation:

Pupils count and record the number of successful catches made in the scoop.

PADDLE BALL

Object: To improve eye-hand coordination.

Equipment: Tennis ball; paddle.

Description:

Students drop a tennis ball on top of a paddle. Each time the ball descends, they hit it up again trying to keep it from touching the floor.

Self-Evaluation:

Pupils count and record the highest number of consecutive hits made.

WAND WHIRL

Object: To improve eye-hand coordination.

Equipment: Wand (two- to three-foot stick).

Description:

Pupils stand the wand upright in front of their bodies. They let go of it, turn quickly and attempt to catch it before it drops to the floor. They must turn alternately left and right with each try.

Self-Evaluation:

Pupils count and record the number of successful catches made.

WAND CATCH

Object: To improve flexibility of legs and eye-hand coordination.

Equipment: Wand.

Description:

Students stand a wand upright with fingers on top. They quickly bring one foot over the stick before it falls. They must step over alternately with the left and right legs.

FIGURE 4-7. Set-up for Wand Catch

Self-Evaluation:

Students count and record the number of successful catches made.

HULA-HOOP JUMPING

Object: To improve cardiovascular fitness and coordination.

Equipment: Hula hoop.

Description:

Students use the hula hoop like a jump rope, jumping forward and backward. When the continuous rhythm of the jump is broken, they begin again.

Self-Evaluation:

Pupils count and record the number of times the continuous rhythm of the jump was broken.

HEAD BALANCE

Object: To improve balance and posture

Equipment: Beanbags (or books).

Description:

Each student places a beanbag on her head, and, without stopping, must walk, stoop, turn, or use some other locomotor movement. If the beanbag falls, the student puts it on her head and begins again. Students should be reminded to stand tall because that stance will help keep the beanbag on the head and will help to improve the posture.

Self-Evaluation:

Pupils count and record the number of times the beanbags fall off their heads.

PUPIL SELF-EVALUATIONS

The teacher should distribute a SELF-TESTING SCORE-CARD to each pupil and explain that students will be recording

ACTIVITY	1 ST DAY	2 ND DAY	3 RD DAY	4 TH DAY	5 TH DAY
CATCH A BALL					
THROUGH THE STICK					
WALK A ROPE					
RUN IN PLACE					
BEAN BAG TOSS					
ONE LEG BALANCE					
HANG OVER DOOR					
SHUTTLE RUN					
BUILDING CHECKERS					
MAKING TENTS					
FORWARD BALANCE					
WRITING BEHIND					
SIT TO STAND					
ARM CIRCLES					
PLAYING DICE					
PADDLE BALL					
WAND WHIRL					
WAND CATCH					
HULA-HOOP JUMPING					
HEAD BALANCE					

FIGURE 4-8. Sample Self-Testing Scorecard for a class of twenty students

their own scores for each activity at the end of the one-minute time period allotted to each.

The children should be encouraged to set goals for themselves by asking the following questions at the end of each physical education period:

1. In how many activities am I improving?
2. In how many activities am I still doing as well as I did the last time?

If children in the lower elementary school grades have difficulty keeping accurate scorecards, the teacher may record the results on one large class chart.

CORRELATING WITH OTHER SUBJECTS

THROUGH THE HOOP

Object: To help students learn the multiplication tables and practice basketball shooting techniques.

Equipment: Two playground balls; question cards with multiplication tables; markers for placement of basket, shooting position and team line-up position.

Description:

Students are divided into two teams. Two students from each team join hands to form a basket. The remaining members of each team line up side by side, fifteen feet from their respective baskets. The teacher lines up between the two baskets with the question cards and the two playground balls.

The teacher selects a card and reads the multiplication problem. Players take turns running to the teacher and whispering

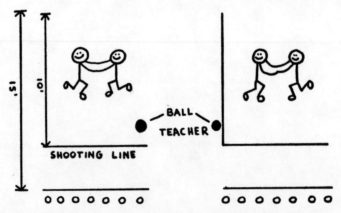

FIGURE 4-9. Playing area for Through the Hoop

the answer. The first student from each team with the correct answer picks up a ball and runs to the shooting line to attempt a basket. The first player to score is awarded two team points.

Students giving an incorrect answer must return to the team line. The next member is then eligible to run up and answer the question provided the opposing team has not already scored. After each attempted basket, the students forming the basket retrieve the ball for the shooter. The two shooters become a part of their respective basket so that different players take turns forming the basket.

Variations:

1. Have players alternate giving the answer.
2. Softball pitching could be used by making a target with a large open circle to pitch through.
3. Other subjects could be used on the question cards. Examples would be:
   English– Parts of speech
   History– Presidents
   Art– Colors
   Health– Symptoms of diseases
   Mathematics– Geometric figures
   Science– Vocabulary definitions
4. Vary the distance and modes of locomotion that are used.

DANCE MY TUNE

Object: To learn about the customs, rituals, and living patterns of another country through representative dances.

Equipment: Record player and records of folk dances from different countries.

Description:

A folk dance series will be scheduled over a period of several weeks. Each student will design a poster depicting one characteristic of the country where one dance originated. These posters will be displayed on the day that the dance is being learned.

Variation:

In home economics or art class, make costumes that are traditional in the country whose dance is being learned.

CONTINENTS

Object: To learn about countries through the games played in those countries. (The games are taught at the time students study about the countries in history or social studies classes.)

Equipment: Implements needed for games of other countries.

Description:

Games that are representative of the country being studied are learned and played.

Variations:

1. Have the students research the games and teach them with the assistance of the teacher.
2. At the beginning of the year, have students write to students in other countries for descriptions of their favorite games that can then be played in class. (Correlate this activity with the English and/or foreign language classes.)
3. It would also be possible to dress for the activity as a person in that country would dress.

SPELLBOUND

Object: To stimulate students to learn how to rhyme words.

Equipment: A set of cards with letters of the alphabet for each team, and a basketball for each team.

Description:

Divide the class into teams and give each team a basketball. Cards with letters of the alphabet on them are placed on the floor.

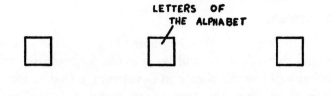

FIGURE 4-10. Set-up for Spellbound

The teacher reads all but the last word of a poem or a saying. Each team must think of a rhyming word to end the sentence. The first person on the team dribbles the basketball to the cards and picks up the first letter of the word that has been selected and dribbles back to the team line. Players alternate dribbling to select a letter until the word is spelled. The first team to complete the spelling of a rhyming word wins the game.

Variation:

Mathematical problems could be used, with numbers instead of letters.

THEME PARK

Object: Students blend their activities in all classes to gain broad comprehension about a theme that has been selected by the teachers.

Equipment: Items needed for the theme that is selected.

Description:

A theme such as the beginning of spring, the solar system, or moving through space will be selected for intensive study. Each teacher will use the theme in developing activities that will allow students to view the topic from many different perspectives. Student as well as teacher creativity should be used to design activities for all classes.

Variation:

The art, music, and physical education teachers can work together on basic themes if the entire school is not involved.

ALPHABET SOUP

Object: To learn the alphabet while developing kinetic awareness with the body.

Equipment: None.

Description:

Each student has a partner. All the letters of the alphabet are placed in a large "soup bowl." Children take turns pulling letters out of the bowl, and each pair forms the letters while lying on the floor.

Variations:

1. Have the students form the letters while sitting or standing.
2. Establish groups of three (or more) and require one student to stand, one to sit, and one to kneel when forming the letters.
3. Put names or pictures of different items to be imitated in the soup bowl; for example, different types of transportation (horse, truck, ship), or complex figures, or pyramids to be formed.

SPELLING SPRINT

Object: To spell selected words and perform different locomotor skills, as well as to develop teamwork and leadership skills.

Equipment: Three sets of alphabet cards.

Description:

The class is divided into three groups of equal size. Each group is given a set of alphabet cards and forms a circle. Each student holds up one card and the remaining cards are placed face up in the circle. The teacher calls out a word for the groups to spell. (Words with two or more of the same letter cannot be used.) Members of the group see if they have the letters needed to spell the word. If they do not, they may exchange their letter for one in their pile. When a team is able to spell the word, the members run to a designated spelling line and hold the letters above their heads to spell the word. Scoring can be on a 5-3-1 (win-tie-loss) basis so that each team scores in every game.

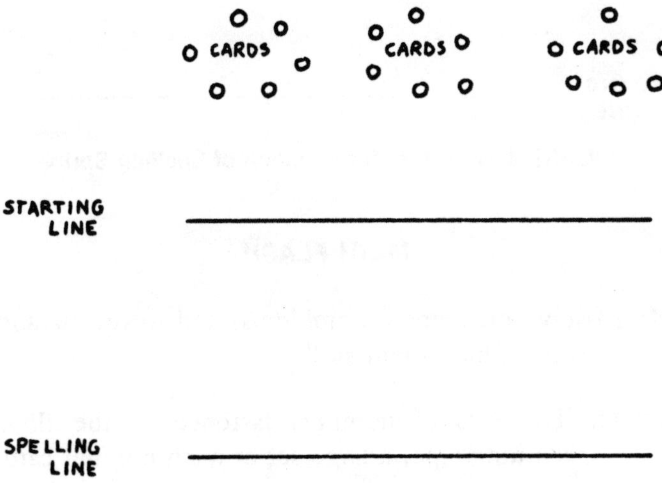

FIGURE 4-11. Playing area for Spelling Sprint

Cards are shuffled and new cards are selected to start each game. Words to use in the game should be obtained from the classroom teacher.

Variations:

1. Different locomotor skills can be used to move from the starting line to the spelling line.
2. Three sets of cards can be placed face down to start the game.
3. Team members must use a designated form of locomotion to go to the pile, pick up a card and return to their team.
4. Team members alternate going to the card pile until they are able to spell the word.

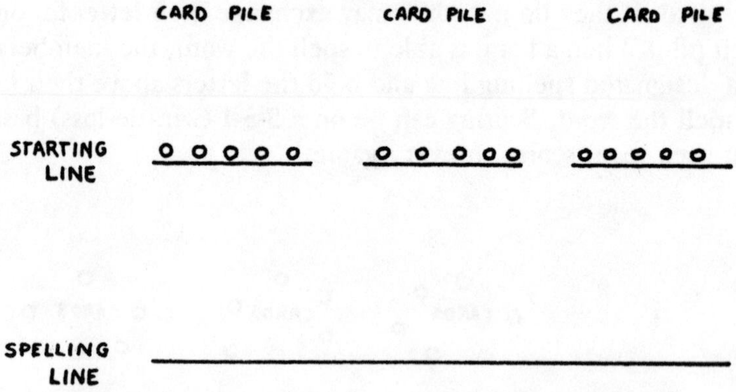

FIGURE 4-12. Set-up for Variation of Spelling Sprint

MATH FLASH

Object: To solve mathematics problems, and to review and reinforce basic movement skills.

Equipment: Two sets of numbers fastened to the floor with masking tape; a large set of math number cards.

Description:

Two teams are formed. Each team has half of the activity area in which to move. It also has one set of numbers fastened randomly on its floor area. On a signal from the teacher, the students move around their team area doing the motor skill indicated by the teacher. After a few minutes, a flash card with a number combination is held up. The students on each team compute the problem individually and then make contact with the number in their activity area that they think is the correct answer.

Variations:

1. The numbers can be mixed over the entire floor and the students can use all the area for movement.

2. Students can suggest the movement that will be used.

JUMP ROPE ARITHMETIC

Object: To practice arithmetic concepts by using a jump rope.

Equipment: Segmented plastic jump ropes.

Description:

The jump rope is used to form geometric shapes that are being learned in class. Shapes can be placed on the floor and the children can place their ropes over the shapes or duplicate the shapes with their ropes. They can also be asked to make larger versions of the shapes they see on the floor.

Variations:

1. Ask the children to make three-, four- or five-sided shapes. Older children can be challenged to form triangles, squares, and other geometric forms.

2. The students can count the number of plastic sections in their ropes.

3. Have the children measure themselves with the rope to see how many pieces tall they are. Older children can use their multiplication skills by multiplying the number of sections by the length of each section.

4. The ropes can be stretched on the floor or ground and the children asked to see how many pieces long they can jump using one leg, two legs, and a running start. They can

either count the pieces or subtract the number of pieces remaining from the total number of pieces of their rope.

5. Children can also form answers to arithmetic problems with their ropes.

THEATRICAL STARDOM

Object: To give students the opportunity to use body movements to express themselves and to reinforce what they are learning in other classes.

Equipment: None.

Description:

Work with the reading teacher and select a story the children are reading. Have the children divide into groups and act out the story. Let the children express themselves through movement.

Variations:

1. Select other subjects and have the children use movement to depict what they are learning in class. For example, if a class is studying how trees grow, the children can begin as small seeds and "grow" into large trees. Then they can be asked to change during each of the seasons.

2. Have the class show how an astronaut moves about on the moon and on various planets when they are studying this unit in science.

CAST A SPELL

Object: To practice spelling words that students are learning in other classes.

Equipment: None.

Description:

This game is to be used after the students have learned how to form letters with their bodies. The class will be formed into groups of five to eight and each group will spell out selected words with their bodies. All members of the group must be used in spelling out the word.

Variations:

1. Have one group demonstrate a word it has chosen and have the other groups guess the word.

2. Have one group put a mathematics problem on the floor by using their bodies and have the other groups compete to form the correct answer. The first group to do this is declared the winner, and gets to put the next problem on the floor.

SPELLING DARTS

Object: To improve throwing skills and hand-eye coordination in conjunction with students' weekly spelling words.

Equipment: A dart board sectioned with all the letters of the alphabet; four conventional-tipped or velcro darts depending on the type of dart board; a box containing a selection of words, all of which have an equal number of letters.

Description:

There should be a maximum of four students to a dart board. Each participant picks one of the spelling words from the box and tries to be the first to spell the selected word by hitting all the letters of the word on the dart board. Each player throws all four darts before the next person throws. The letters must be hit in sequence. After all players have thrown, the rotation starts again. The first player to cross out all the letters and spell the word is the winner.

Variations:

1. Have the students spell the same word.

2. Have numbers instead of letters on the dart board and see who can correctly solve mathematics problems.

H	A	J	C	V
U	PENALTY	D	PENALTY	B
Q	I	FREE LETTER	B	Z
R	O	N	T	E
G	P	F	S	MISS
Y	M	MISS	L	W

SAMPLE WORDS:

MARK   FISH   SWIM
LEFT

FIGURE 4-13. Sample dartboard for Spelling Darts

ALPHABET SPELLING RACE

Object: To practice spelling words and gain experience in being assertive when reaching for the correct letters.

Equipment: Cards with letters of the alphabet on them for each team (there should be two of each vowel and two T's, R's and L's); a list of spelling words drawn from different subjects.

Description:

The captain of each team comes forward to the teacher who whispers a word to each of them. On the teacher's signal, the captains will run to their respective teams. Each member of the team holds several letters. The captains will pull those teammates holding the appropriate letters to a designated area to spell the word. The first team to spell the word correctly wins a team point. A new captain is picked for each word and the former captain takes the place of one of the letter-holding players.

Variation:

Have the captain take the correct cards from teammates and run to spell the word by laying the letters on the floor. Only one letter may be moved each trip. Different locomotor movements may be required when taking the card to spell the word.

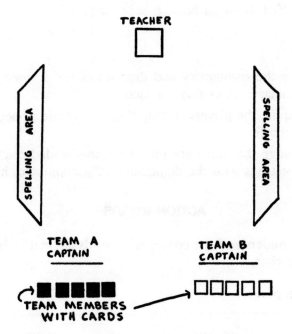

FIGURE 4-14. Set-up for Alphabet Spelling Race.

FIVE DOLLARS

Object: To practice throwing and catching skills. To develop arithmetic skills in a physical education setting.

Equipment: Any ball appropriate for throwing and catching.

Description:

Members of the class are divided into groups of three or four. One player in each group is the leader. The others stand side by side facing the leader. The leader throws the ball to each player in turn. The players catch the ball and return the throw. Each player tries to earn $5.00 and become the leader.

Scoring

1. Successful catch on the fly–$1.00
2. Successfull catch on one bounce–$.50
3. Dropped throw–subtract $1.00
4. Muffed throw on bounce–subtract $.50

Variations:

1. Vary the complexity and distance of the throws and the monetary values that are used.
2. Require the players to keep their feet inside a hoop placed on the floor.
3. Change the monetary values for one-handed catches and for catches with the dominant and nondominant hands.

ACTION WORDS

Object: To understand the concepts of words learned in language arts class.

Equipment: None.

Description:

The language arts teacher and the physical education teacher select words that can be expressed with movement. These words are given to the students and they move to show the meaning that each word has for them. Through movement, they are able to develop a better understanding of the meaning of the words.

ALPHABET MEMORIZATION

Object: To review the letters of the alphabet and become familiar with new words.

Equipment: A ball for each group.

Description:

The students form a circle. The student with the ball rolls it to another player who gives a word that begins with the letter A. The next person gives a word that starts with the letter B. This procedure continues until Z is the letter reached.

Variation:

When learning the alphabet, players can call out letters in sequence as they pass the ball. Each person who catches the ball calls out a word that starts with A. This continues until someone is stumped. The team then moves to the letter B and the process is repeated. This can be a noncompetitive game or, with older children, score can be kept and the person who is stumped the fewest times wins the game. A three- to five-second time limit to think of a word should be used as children become proficient.-

5

This Sure Is Different!

Over 30 Change-of-Pace Ideas

TEACHER

STUDENT

This chapter differs from the preceding chapters in that it will not include descriptions of new games and variations. Instead, it will be devoted to ideas that you can use to bring about the change of pace that your class needs to maintain interest and stimulate additional enthusiasm. Needless to say, we are all faced with the situation in which our students seem to have reached a plateau and there seems to be dwindling interest in the scheduled activity. If we were coaching an athletic team, we would probably say that the team was stale. In a coaching situation we would change the emphasis, shorten the practice, or use a new practice drill. Many techniques can also be used in a physical education class to provide a change of pace and restore vitality to a class.

It should be emphasized that a change-of-pace activity can be needed even if you have an outstanding physical education curriculum. The climate, the time of the year, happenings in other classes, school activities, and home influences are all factors that operate in the lives of our students and might affect their mental set as well as their physical vitality. In all likelihood, combinations of factors are at work. Be alert for the telltale signs of lack of alertness, of simply going through the motions, and tap your reservoir of ideas to provide the change of pace that will make physical education fun for you and your students.

Change-of-pace activities can take several different forms. They can be used for a brief period in each class on either a short- or long-term basis. Many teachers have found that a change-of-pace activity can be used effectively during every class. It provides the variety that many children need and it is particularly good to heighten the element of anticipation which is so important to maintain interest. More commonly, a change-of-pace activity is used for an entire class period at selected times during the semester. This different experience will break the monotony that may have been building and result in your students returning to the next class meeting with renewed enthusiasm.

Another alternative is to introduce an entirely new unit that may last three or four weeks or more. The new unit should be completely different from the activity your children have been learning.

It doesn't matter what format your change of pace will take. In this book you will find ideas and activities to fit your needs. Change-of-pace activities, games, and ideas can be found in every chapter. Try something different. You will be amazed at the effect such an approach will have on your students and on your entire approach to teaching. Change the pace to keep pace with student needs!

NEW AND MODIFIED GAMES AND ACTIVITIES

1. As has already been mentioned, hundreds of new games and game modifications are included in this book. There are several different ways that you can find a game that will be appropriate for you. At the beginning of the school year, skim through the book and mark those games you want to try. Then, when you need a change of pace, you can rapidly find an appropriate game by reviewing those you had previously marked.

   Another technique would be to check in the tables of contents in this book or our previous book, *What Are We Doing in Gym Today?* * For example, you might want to have a short activity such as a relay. Refer to a chapter on relays. If you want a dance activity, a new movement format, or a mass game, flip to the appropriate chapter.

   Most of the games and activities that are provided for you throughout the book are appropriate as change-of-pace activities. They were chosen because they are different, they include different skill elements, and they place a strong emphasis on maximum participation and doing things with a new twist. These are exactly the ingredients that make change-of-pace days successful.

2. Select several games and have your students rotate from game to game on a five-to seven-minute schedule. Choose games that require a minimum set-up.

3. Competitive pyramid building is a great change-of-pace activity. It is preferable to build the pyramids on mats or on a grassy area outside. The first lesson should be devoted to pyramid design and to an explanation of various techniques

---

*Kenneth G. Tillman and Patricia Rizzo Toner. *What Are We Doing in Gym Today?* (West Nyack, NY: Parker Publishing Co., Inc., 1983).

for lifting and holding. The lifting and holding techniques should also be demonstrated and practiced thoroughly before the students begin to build pyramids. All students will soon be cognizant of the fact that in pyramid building there is an important place for everyone regardless of ability or size.

After learning the basic techniques, group the students into threes and have them experiment with various three-person pyramids. They should be encouraged to discover different types and shapes of pyramids. One class period is usually sufficient to work on three-person pyramids. The next challenge is to divide the class into groups of twelve to fifteen and have each group design a pyramid. The culmination of this unit is to have each group demonstrate its pyramid to the teacher and the class and have the teacher rate each pyramid. To increase interest, invite parents, administrators, and/or other students to watch the pyramid demonstration.

FIGURE 5-1.

After the students have completed their pyramids, have a race to see which group can move its pyramid across the finish line the fastest. If the pyramid falls apart, it must be rebuilt on the same spot before moving forward.

4. Schedule a modified pentathlon for your classes. Use point totals for each event so that your students will have to compute their own scores.

5. Schedule a free day. Let the students use any piece of equipment that you have available and play any game that has previously been covered in class.

6. Develop a cooperative unit with teachers from other disciplines. One enjoyable technique is to select a common theme and have each discipline relate its activities to that theme. For example, a Colonial America theme would lend itself to learning games and dances of the Colonial period.

7. Look in Chapter 2 for New Twist games. This is a rich resource for change-of-pace ideas.

DIFFERENT IDEAS

1. Have your class play several different games after dividing it into teams. Keep a cumulative total of the scores of all the games that were played to determine the winner at the end of the class period. Scores can be determined by the greatest number of points scored, the fewest points permitted, or the greatest difference between points scored and points permitted.

2. Designate a competitive game for the class to play and then have your students develop a way to play that game cooperatively. Let each team devise a cooperative strategy, and give the class an opportunity to play each variation.

3. Incorporate different aspects of adventure activities into your class. Even one day of working on simulated mountain climbing can be a great change of pace and, as a possible byproduct, it might provide the impetus to start a full-fledged adventure program. Many other adventure skills are appropriate as change-of-pace activities—initiative games, map and compass reading, cross country skiing, backpacking, and hiking techniques, for example.

4. Schedule a field day for the entire school. Instead of standard activities, use only "ridiculous" activities. Have the students assist in designing the "ridiculous" events, and have each class compete as a unit to increase enthusiasm.

5. Let the students design new games on an individual or group basis, and have the entire class try out all the games that have been designed.

6. Have your students design a bulletin board. They should have advance notice so they can bring materials to class. It would be good to have a planning period and then a

FIGURE 5-2.

construction period. The bulletin board project should relate to the activities in class. For example, if you are having a jogging unit, the display might incorporate a mileage chart for individuals, teams, or the entire class.

7. Schedule a field trip that relates to the material being covered in class. This might involve seeing a professional basketball game during your basketball unit, or visiting a museum exhibition that includes information about a sport in your curriculum. Field trips are a rich resource for the innovative physical education teacher. Always follow up with a written observation by your students for maximum benefit.

FIGURE 5-3.

8. Schedule a series of mini-courses at a time when you anticipate that your program will need a lift. A mini-course may last for a day, a week, or two weeks. Use community recources, including parents who have specialized skills that can be shared with your students.

9. Schedule a sport information quiz. With younger students, have them act out answers through movement. Your older students will enjoy the challenge of answering questions covering many different sports.

10. Have a day when students must use their nondominant hands and legs while playing games.

11. Institute a walking program. Contact the Presidents' Council on Physical Fitness and Sports for model programs and information about free walking booklets. You can teach proper walking techniques and involve your students in a fitness program based on brisk walking.

TEACHING METHODOLOGY

1. Bring a videotape recorder to class and tape the students during a game or activity. The tape can be viewed immediately or it can be watched on another date when you again want a change of pace. In addition to providing an excellent change of pace, the videotape is a fine teaching tool. Students are able to see their mistakes and gain insights into how they can correct them.

2. A videotape player can be used effectively to provide instruction when teaching a new skill. This change-of-pace approach can be used to stimulate student interest.

3. Let the students teach. The age of the students will determine the parameters that will need to be established and the degree of assistance that you will give. You might divide the class into small groups and have a student teach each group, or you may want to let several students act as the teachers for the entire class. Consider making this a regular change-of-pace activity and rotate the responsibility so every student has an opportunity to be the teacher.

4. Design task sheets for each of your students. Have them spend one or more class periods completing the indicated task and recording the results. Tasks can range from peforming various skills to peer teaching to researching a favorite game.

5. Let the students make some of the decisions about the class. For example, let them select how warm-ups will be conducted. You might also want to let them determine the instructional approach that you will use. Will your class be structured or very informal? Gradually increase your students' participation in the decision-making process.

6. Join in the activity yourself. It is great if you can get other teachers and administrators to participate also.

7. Use films or film strips if you don't already use them on a regular basis.

8. Vary your class management techniques. Take attendance differently or use a different procedure to organize your class for the day's activities.

9. Let your students make up their own games. They can do this during a class period or they can devise a game out of class to play during a specified class period.

10. If you teach in a cold climate, surprise your students and take them outside during snowy weather. There are many fine snow games that are never used in physical education classes because we stay indoors when snow is on the ground.

11. Use a tape recording to give directions to your class. Have a mystery voice give the directions. Also, let students alternate responsibilities for taping some sessions.

12. Use background music for your classes. Your students will enjoy selecting the music. Using music to establish the tempo for your activities can be a fine change-of-pace technique.

13. Establish a series of learning stations in your gymnasium. Use several stations and rotate your students from station to station to keep the level of anticipation high. If you frequently use learning stations, have surprise activities at each station for a week. Use novel and slightly crazy stunts and challenges.

6

Raindrops Keep Fallin' on My Head

40 Activities to Brighten
Your Rainy Days

Rainy days can be dreary days for the elementary teacher and the physical education teacher. The overcast sky and confinement contribute to this feeling. The physical education teacher is faced with an added problem when an outdoor class has to be moved indoors suddenly because of rain. The problem is further complicated when this move puts more than one class in an area normally assigned to a single class. It is at times like this when you need rainy day games to brighten your day!

No doubt you have rainy day lesson plans ready. The games in this chapter can be used to fit into your current plans or they can be used to develop alternate rainy day plans. In either case, they provide you with resources to maintain class excitement.

You will note that the games in this chapter involve a lot of action and movement. A rainy day contributes to student restlessness. Students need games that involve physical exertion and provide the challenge to keep them mentally immersed in the activity. The games in this chapter have these ingredients.

You will find that these activities are not merely time killers. They have educational value, meet physical education objectives, and are fun. Set them up in keeping with your typical lesson plan format and you can move smoothly into your lesson even when you have to make a sudden move indoors without time for advance planning.

We want your rainy day activities to cause your students to look forward to their physical education class, not to groan that it is raining and that class will be dull. We also encouage you to use these activities to reduce the discipline problems that frequently crop up on a rainy day. If your students get involved in games that challenge them, they soon forget the weather and key in on the activity instead.

We also encourage you to look through the other chapters in this book and select games and activities that you would like to use specifically for rainy days. If you live in a climate that has many cloudy days, you may find it helpful to select numerous activities. This will provide the necessary variety in your rainy day program. Activities need to be changed and new activities introduced frequently to overcome the problem of motivating students on rainy days.

You must make the best possible use of your indoor facilities during inclement weather. The games and activities in this chapter are designed with this in mind. Your rainy days can be among your most enjoyable and eagerly anticipated days if you make wise use of the ideas presented in this chapter and in the other chapters of this book.

DOUBLE CROSS

Object: To pull the opposing team across the restraining line.

Equipment: Wrestling mat; tape or chalk.

Description:

Divide the class in half and position the teams facing one another on either side of the tape or chalk line. On a signal, each team attempts to pull the other team across the line. If a player is pulled across, he or she must sit in a designated scoring area. Players may step one foot over the line, but if both feet are across at any one time, the player is captured. The team with the fewest captured players is the winner.

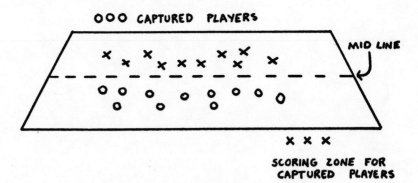

FIGURE 6-1. Set-up for Double Cross

HOPPIN' MAD

Object: To cause the opponent to cross the restraining line.

Equipment: Wrestling mat; tape or chalk.

Description:

Assign the students to pairs. Each player, standing on opposite sides of a tape or chalk line, grasps the opponent's right hand and, hopping on his right foot, attempts to pull the opponent over the line. Either contestant loses if he touches the rear foot to the ground. The first to win three bouts wins the match.

Variations:

1. Alternate hands and feet.
2. Set up a time for players to challenge other players and determine a class champion.
3. Play team competition, whereby the team with the most individual champions is the winner.

BACK-UP

Object: To push the opponent over the base line.

Equipment: Mat; tape or chalk.

Description:

Have two contestants stand back to back with elbows locked, right arm inside the opponent's left arm. Place a base line ten feet in front of each contestant. At the signal, each player, by pushing backward, attempts to force the opponent over the base line. Lifting and carrying are not permitted. The first to win three bouts is the winner.

BASE LINE

FIGURE 6-2. Playing area for Back-Up

KNEE TAG

Object: To tag an opponent's knee, thereby scoring points.

Equipment: One fifteen-inch piece of rope for every set of partners.

Description:

Each partner holds one end of a rope. On a given signal, each player tries to tag his or her opponent's knee with the free hand, without letting go of the rope with the other hand. One point is scored each time one partner tags her opponent's knee.

Variations:

1. Use different lengths of rope.
2. Play in a sectioned-off area of the mat or playground without using the ropes.

CROSSE-BALL

Object: To score by getting the ball in the goal.

Equipment: Yarn ball (or cotton packed and wrapped with adhesive tape); badminton rackets; baseball gloves (optional).

Description:

Divide the class into teams of twelve to fifteen. Two teams play on the court at once. Players transport the ball on their rackets as they run, or they may pass the ball by tossing it and striking it with the racket. Players must stay in their respective zones. There are three zones—defense, mid-field, and attack. Checking may only be done by hitting your opponent's racket face with your racket face. (NOTE: Checking can be eliminated altogether if desired.) A loose ball may be secured by picking it up with the glove hand or non-racket hand. Opponents may try to take the ball away but only with their non-racket hands and not with the rackets. Any shots on goal must be taken from outside the crease. If goals are not available, an area designated as goal can be taped to the wall.

Since the game is designed to be played indoors, anything off the walls is playable except for the sideline where other teams are seated. For any rule infraction, a free shot on goal is taken from in front of the crease by the offended team. The goalie in crosse-ball must stay within the crease and will put all unsuccessful shots back into play by hitting the ball out. The ball cannot be thrown.

Rule infractions are listed below:

1. Checking below the face of the opponent's racket.
2. Any unsafe play such as striking the ball when another player is close enough to be hit.
3. Tripping, pushing, shoving, or any other unsportsmanlike conduct.

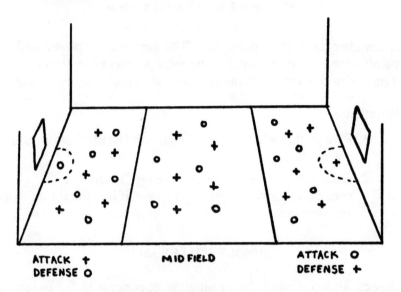

ATTACK +   MID FIELD   ATTACK O
DEFENSE O   DEFENSE +

FIGURE 6-3. Crosse-Ball court

COIN TOSS

Object: To toss a coin into the scoring areas of the coin toss target.

Equipment: Any coins; target made of cardboard, wood, or drawn with chalk.

Description:

Divide the class into equal teams of up to five players, and number the players from one to five. Have each team toss against another team, or against the clock, or have players toss against each other. In the team-against-team version, the team members toss in numerical order, alternating with the opposing team, attempting to

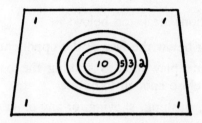

FIGURE 6-4. Coin Toss target area

accumulate the highest point total. The game can be played to fifty points or to see which team has the most points in one class period. Target size can vary with the ages and skill levels of the students.

Variations:

1. Play so that when the coin lands on "heads," point values are doubled.
2. Give players the option of calling "heads" or "tails." If correct, point values are tripled, but if incorrect, no points are awarded.

JUNGLE VOLLEYBALL

Object: To score points by causing the opponents to fail to return the volleyball before it hits the floor twice.

Equipment: Volleyball; standards; volleyball net lowered to floor level.

Description:

Divide the class into equal teams and assign each to a court. The ball is served over the net and is played on the fly or after a bounce. The ball may bounce off the bleachers, beams, basketball standards or any other obstruction, and still be in play. The players may use as many hits per side as necessary in order to return the ball to the opponent's court. Players may use set-ups, spikes, or any other hand contact with the ball to send it over the net. The ball must be hit over the net and between the standards, and must touch a player before it bounces on the floor for a second time.

(This does not include the wall, the bleachers, etc.) No player may hit the ball twice in succession. The serve must clear the net.

Points are awarded to the serving side only. The game may be played up to fifteen points or until a time limit is reached.

Variations:

1. Use tennis courts and set up strict boundaries.
2. Use a larger enclosed area such as half of a gym.
3. Allow assists on the serve.
4. Raise the net to regulation volleyball height.

DODGE BASEBALL

Object: To avoid being hit by the ball in order to cross home plate and score runs.

Equipment: Bases; foam rubber ball or rubber playground ball.

Description:

Divide the class into two teams and set up as in softball. The pitcher stands fifteen feet from home plate and delivers the ball in an easy underhand fashion. The fielding team spreads out across the entire playing area. Once the ball is hit with the hand, the batter runs to as many bases as possible without being hit by a thrown ball. Once on a base, the runner is safe and cannot be hit by the ball. A runner does not have to leave the base and any number of runners may share the same base. An out is scored only when the runner is struck with the ball below the waist while not on base. The only guaranteed score is a home run which would be a ball hit against the far wall above the halfway mark. Each team is allowed six outs per inning. The team with the most runs wins the game.

VOLLEY-BOUNCE-BALL

Object: To score points by causing the other team to miss the ball.

Equipment: One playground ball; volleyball court or full gym depending on skill level and age of participants (the area must have a center line and boundaries).

Description:

Volley-Bounce-Ball is similar to volleyball but is played without a net. Divide the class into teams of up to fifteen and start play with a volley to determine which team will serve. The serving side must drop or bounce the ball onto the floor and then serve to its own forward line. The forward line then hits the ball over the center line to the opposing team. The receiving side has three hits in which to return the ball and may let the ball bounce on the floor one time. The rules include the following:

1. Players may not spike the ball.
2. Players may not cross the center line.
3. The ball may be hit with the hands only.
4. Rotation is used so that all members of a team can serve.
5. Points are awarded when errors are made by the receiving team.
6. Only the serving side can score.
7. The game is won when one team has eleven points and is two ahead of the opponents.

Variations:

1. Play a time-limit game and the team with the most points at the end of the designated time is the winner.

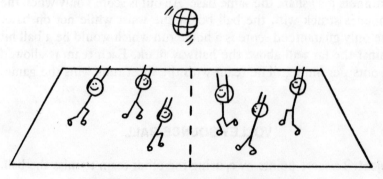

FIGURE 6-5. Volley-Bounce-Ball court

2. Allow more advanced teams to spike the ball and permit two bounces on the floor per team for each point.

SHARPSHOOTER

Object: To circle the bases before the opposing team can make three passes and make a basket.

Equipment: Bases and one playground ball.

Description:

Divide the class into two teams. The fielding team is spread around the floor with two team members designated as sharpshooters. (Change the sharpshooters with every batter so all have a chance.)

Members of the batting team hit the ball with their fists from a drop position or a held position. The fielding team must then

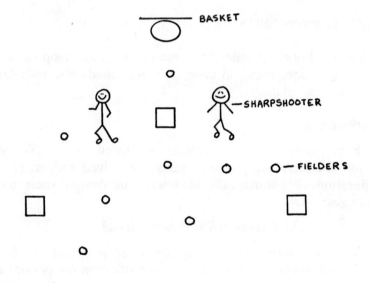

FIGURE 6-6. Sharpshooter playing area

make three passes to three different players and toss the ball to the sharpshooters who try to make a basket before the batter circles the bases. The batters score one point for their team each time they circle the bases. Teams change positions after three baskets (outs) are made. Shooters may not pass to each other and all passes must be complete or the count must start over.

Variations:

1. Specify the types of passes and shots to be made.
2. Require all fielders to receive a pass before giving the ball to a sharpshooter and allow the runner to count one point for each time the bases are circled before the basket is made.
3. Require the shooters to make two or more baskets.

PROBLEM CHILD

Object: To successfully solve group problems.

Equipment: Ropes; parallel bars; mats; tent; hula hoop or milk crate; tires; tin cans; 2 × 4's; blindfolds; volleyball standard.

Description:

Some sample group problems are listed below. No one solution is correct and problems cannot be solved without group cooperation. Students may also wish to design their own challenges.

Problem 1: The Poisoned Marsh

Transport your entire group across the poisoned marsh as quickly as possible. Only the tin cans are safe from the poison; all other objects are destroyed by the poison. If a player falls into the poisoned marsh, he or she must return to the starting point. If the poisoned player is touching any other players when he or she falls in, all those touched are poisoned and must return also.

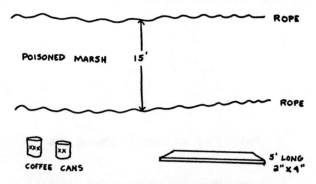

FIGURE 6-7. Diagram of The Poisoned Marsh

Problem 2: The Elephant

Set up the parallel bars or beam and mats as shown in Figure 6-8. Transport your team over the elephant as quickly as possible.

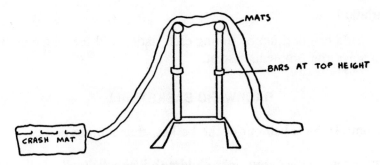

FIGURE 6-8. Set-up for The Elephant

Problem 3: Now You See It

Have one person who is not blindfolded direct blindfolded persons to complete a task such as setting up a tent or building a pyramid of empty boxes.

Problem 4: All Included

Try to fit as many people as possible into a hula hoop placed on the ground, or as many as possible on top of a milk crate.

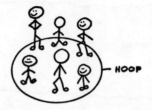

FIGURE 6-9. All Included playing area

Problem 5: Ring the Pole

Try to get three tires over the top and down the volleyball standard as quickly as possible. The standard must remain perpendicular to the floor at all times and no player may touch the standard base at any time.

These activities provide a great rainy day challenge. Stations can be set up so that groups can rotate to each problem solving area.

Variation:

Add competition by timing each station and see which groups can solve the problems fastest.

BACKWARD BASKETBALL

Object: To hit a ball out of the basket, thus scoring points.

Equipment: Two lightweight children's kickballs (volleyball size); one small playground ball; string to tie up bottoms of basketball nets; basketball court.

Description:

Divide the class into teams of up to eight players. The game is played like basketball except that to score, players must knock a kickball out of tied-up basketball nets. A kickball is placed in each tied-up basket at the start of the game, and the balls are returned to the baskets each time a team scores. Each time the ball is knocked out, a point is scored. The game is started with a center jump and once the ball is in play it must be passed from team member to team member, or it may be run with for up to three seconds before

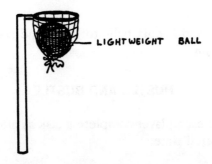

LIGHTWEIGHT BALL

FIGURE 6-10. Backwards Basketball net diagram

it must be passed or shot. A tie ball requires a center jump. For all rule infractions, the ball is awarded to the opposing team on the sidelines.

Rule infractions

1. Players holding the ball longer than three seconds.
2. Unsportsmanlike conduct.

CONE BASEBALL

Object: To score runs by crossing home plate.

Equipment: One cone per player; tennis ball; wiffle ball bat.

Description:

The rules and set-up for cone baseball are the same as those for regular baseball with two exceptions: rather than using gloves, players must catch the ball in the cones and batters must hit the ball off the "tee" cone. Players may throw the ball by hand but it always must be caught with the cone.

FIGURE 6-11. Cone Baseball playing area

Variation:

Use cones and tennis balls to play cone soccer, basketball, football and so on.

HUSTLE AND BUSTLE

Object: To have each player complete a task as often as possible in the allotted time.

Equipment: Basketball and basket; rope; paddle and tennis ball; eight tires; six cones; four hurdles; tin can; volleyball; wall target; score sheets; direction cards; stop watch.

Description:

Set up stations as described or set up your own challenges. Divide the class into equal groups, assign each group to a starting station, and give each group a score card. Each time a group member completes the task at a station, the group scores one point. Group members take turns until time is up. Rotate the groups among all the stations; total each team's points and announce the winners. Sample stations might include:

Station 1: Run through the tires and back to the starting line. Each tire must be touched.

Station 2: Hit the ball above the line three times with a paddle. Score one point for every three hits.

Station 3: Zig-zag up and back through the cones.

Station 4: Shoot a basket and score one point for each successful shot. After three tries, if no basket is made, give the ball to the next player.

Station 5: Jump rope ten times and score one point for every ten jumps.

Station 6: Volley the ball on the wall four times above an eight-foot line. Score one point for every four volleys.

Station 7: Pass under the first hurdle, over the second, under the third, and over the fourth and run back.

Station 8: Using only one foot, pick up the tin can, hop to the line and give it to the next player without using hands. Score one point each time your team crosses a starting line with the tin can.

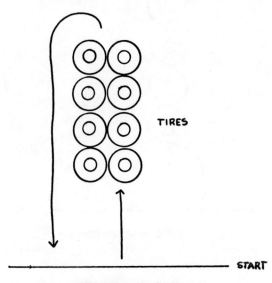

FIGURE 6-12. Station 1

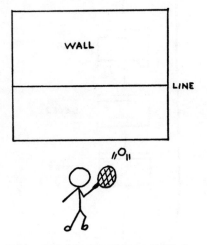

FIGURE 6-13. Station 2

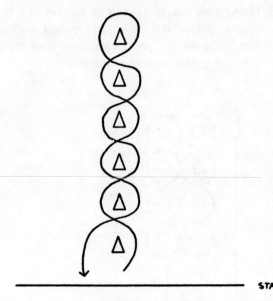

START

FIGURE 6-14. Station 3

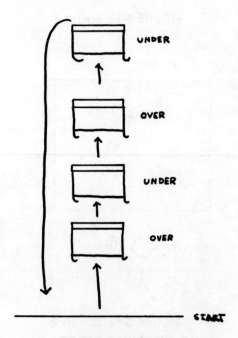

UNDER

OVER

UNDER

OVER

START

FIGURE 6-15. Station 7

STATION 8.

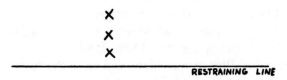

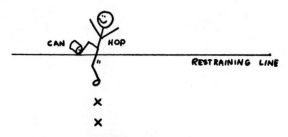

FIGURE 6-16. Station 8

WALL BALL

Object: To hit the other team's wall below a marked line.

Equipment: Four playground balls; taped lines four feet from floor.

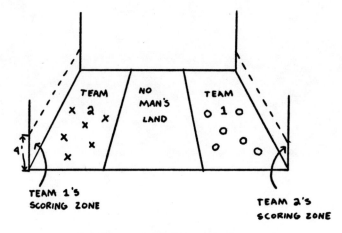

FIGURE 6-17. Wall Ball playing area

Description:

Divide the class into two teams and divide the gym into three sections. Place the teams in their respective sections as shown in Figure 6-17. The players attempt to score goals by hitting the opponent's wall below the taped line. Each hit scores a goal and is worth one point. Players may block and catch the balls but no one is allowed in "no-man's-land." The first team to score ten points is the winner.

7

Happy Holidaze

47 Ways to Make
Your Holidays Dazzle

As holidays approach, the excitement level rises in your classes. Children anticipate a day off or an extended vacation. They find it difficult to think about classwork. Physical education is no different from any other subject. Student concentration deteriorates, and the learning that takes place frequently approaches point zero. Class control problems increase, and children's thoughts stray easily. It is for these exasperating times that we have written this chapter. The old adage, "if you can't beat them, join them," applies. We have included numerous activities that can be used for the holidays that occur during the school year. Capitalize on the student interest that is generated by a holiday. Select one or more of the activities in this chapter for the holiday that is approaching. You already have your students' interest. Let the games do the rest to give you an enjoyable and productive physical education class.

Many of the activities are appropriate to be used jointly with teachers of other subjects. For example, holiday games make extensive use of art materials. Patriotic games have tremendous potential as a joint project with social studies teachers. The more you relate the holiday activities to what is occurring in other classes, as well as at home and in the community, the more valuable your classes will be and the more your students will learn.

Holiday games can also be used to heighten students' awareness of the significance of some of the lesser-known holidays. As holidays approach, give out-of-class assignments that ask students to obtain background information about the holiday. In some instances, it might be helpful to structure your questions to include the concepts and/or meanings of some of the games.

Another thing you should consider is the use of student ideas for holiday activities. Different cultures and ethnic groups have games that are traditionally used for different holidays. Let your children share these games as you move into your holiday seasons. Parents should also be used as resources. Send a request home for games that they have used for specific holidays. You will find that some parents will be willing to come to class and assist you in teaching holiday games. Parents are particularly good resources for traditional musical games and dances. This kind of activity is perfect for your holiday physical education classes.

Make your holiday seasons the highlight of your physical education year by capitalizing on the excitement they generate.

LABOR DAY RELAY

Object: To match the word with the description of the occupation as quickly as possible.

Equipment: Occupation cards or picture cards placed in a hula hoop; description cards.

Description:

Divide the class into teams of equal size, and hand each team member a card with a description of an occupation on it (description card). On the signal, one team member at a time must run to the hula hoop containing the occupation cards, find the card that

FIGURE 7-1. Sample Occupation and Description Cards

matches the job description, and place it in his team's scoring zone outside the hoop. That player then runs back to the line and tags the next player who must do the same. Play continues until all cards are matched. The first team to finish receives three points, the second two points, and the third one point. Each team that correctly matches all cards also receives one point.

Depending on the age level of the students, the cards can progress from simple picture cards to more difficult word descriptions.

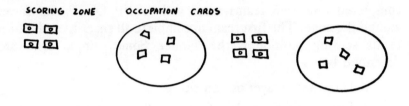

FIGURE 7-2. Playing area for Labor Day Relay

Variation:

Place the names of famous persons in the hoop and have students match them with their occupations. (For example, Walter Reed—Bacteriologist; Augustus Caesar—first Emperor of the Roman World.)

SHAPE UP AND SHIP OUT (COLUMBUS DAY)

Object: To be the first team to complete the tasks and "ship out."

Equipment: Six task cards per team; cones; ropes; mats.

Description:

Divide the class into teams of equal size, and give each team a packet of numbered task cards. On a signal, task #1 is completed by every team member. When all are finished, the group yells, "SHIP OUT." At this time, they must join hands and form a chain, run around the cone, and return to their starting area and the task cards. Each person then performs task #2 and so on. After each completed task, the teams must yell "SHIP OUT" and travel around the cone. The first team to complete all six tasks and return to its starting position is the winner. Some sample tasks are described below:

1. Have each player do ten sit-ups.
2. Have each player do a forward roll, one at a time.
3. Have each player do twenty jumping jacks.
4. Have each player do three tuck jumps.
5. Have each player jump rope five times. (Provide only one rope.)
6. Have each player do ten push-ups.

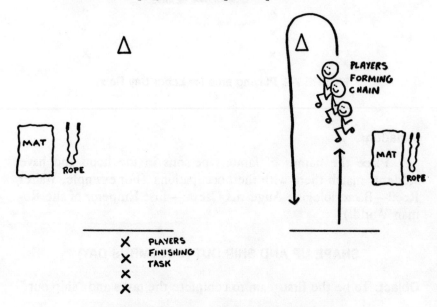

FIGURE 7-3. Set-up for Shape Up and Ship Out

Variation:

Have the tasks relate to a particular unit being studied. For example, in a volleyball unit, the skills could include setting, spiking, serving at a target, etc.

WATER BRIGADE (FIRE PREVENTION WEEK)

Object: To have the most water in the bucket at the end of the game.

Equipment: Two buckets per line; one small paper cup per player.

Description:

Divide the class into squads of equal size in single file formation. Place a bucket in front of and behind each line. Fill all the buckets in the front of the lines with water, making sure they are all filled to the same depth. The buckets at the end of the lines remain empty. On a signal, the first player in each line fills the cup from the bucket and pours that water into the next player's cup and so on, until it reaches the last player. The last player pours the water into the empty bucket and runs to the front of the line to begin the process again. The game continues until the front bucket is empty.

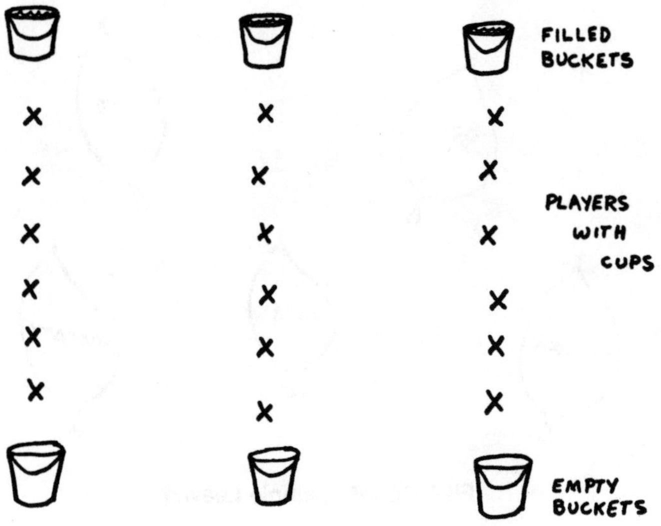

FIGURE 7-4. Set-up for Water Brigade

The winning team is the team with the most water in the bucket at the end of its line. Points can also be awarded for the first team finished. It is advisable to play this game outdoors in a grassy area, for obvious reasons.

LEAF ME ALONE (FIRST DAY OF FALL–AUTUMNAL EQUINOX)

Object: To capture as many leaves as possible.

Equipment: One construction paper leaf per player; a paper bag to hold the leaves.

Description:

Have all the players choose a leaf from the bag without talking. All leaves should be marked with a word or symbol but only two leaves should match. On a signal, the players walk around

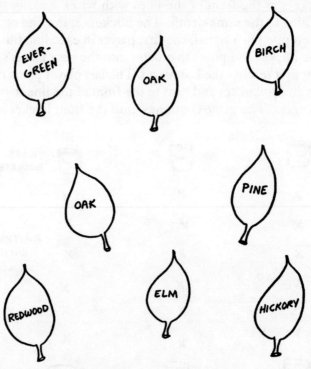

FIGURE 7-5. Sample Leaves

trying to find a player whose leaf matches theirs. When the two players find each other, they just join hands and tag as many others as they can with their free hands. Once a leaf is captured, it must join the chain on the outside and tag the others. Before joining the chain, the tagged player drops the leaf into the paper bag. The last leaf left is the winner.

Variations:

1. Use any subject area when labeling the leaves; matching answers to math problems, spelling words, or other combinations.

2. Have all the leaves match and let the students find their match. The game can be made competitive by seeing which leaves match first.

3. Also, there can be one or two unmatched leaves and the children with these leaves can mix the leaves for the next game.

GHOST ROAST (HALLOWEEN)

Object: To be the first team to complete the assigned tasks.

Equipment: Candle and holder; matches (to be carefully supervised by the instructor); ghost cards in the shape of ghosts (locomotor movements are printed on the cards beforehand in evaporated milk which will be invisible when dry).

Description:

Form a large circle with the players sitting Indian-style on the floor. Divide the circle into four equal sections and give each team member a number from one to ?. The teacher sits in the center of the circle with the lighted candle (it is advisable to have a bucket of water nearby) and the ghost cards. To begin the game, the #1s from each team stand facing in a counterclockwise direction. A member of the first team goes to the center of the circle, chooses a ghost card and very carefully holds it over the flame (milk side down). The flame causes the evaporated milk to become visible.

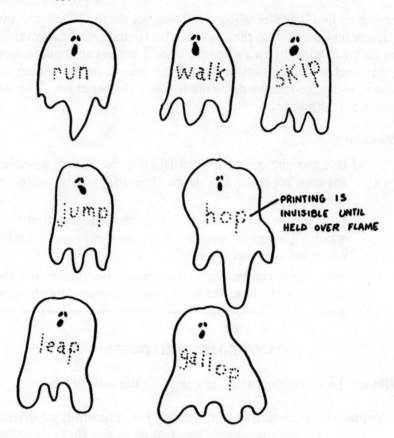

FIGURE 7-6. Sample Ghost Roast Cards

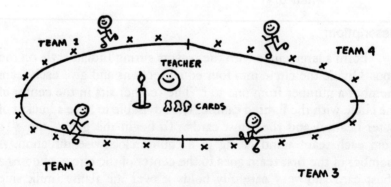

FIGURE 7-7. Ghost Roast set-up

When the word describing a locomotor movement appears on the card, the center player calls out the movement and the four standing players must use that movement to go around the circle and back to their original spots. The first player back receives a point for his or her team. Continue until all players have had a turn. Alternate the ghost card readers from each team.

BAT IN A CAVE (HALLOWEEN)

Object: To find an unoccupied cave as a home for Halloween night.

Equipment: None.

Description:

Divide the class into groups of four. Three of the players should join hands as shown in Figure 7-8 to form a cave. The fourth player stands in the middle and is the bat. One child in the class is designated as the bat without a home. On a starting signal, all bats must leave their caves and find a new home. The bat left without a cave then starts the next round. Give each player an opportunity to be a bat and a cave.

FIGURE 7-8. Set-up for Bat in a Cave

Variation:

Play Bat in a Cave as you would musical chairs. When the music starts, all bats must leave their caves and wander until the music stops. At that time they must each try to find an unoccupied cave. Play records of Halloween horror sounds or songs such as Saint-Saëns' "Danse Macabre" or Mussorgsky's *Night on Bald Mountain* for added effect.

WHICH WITCH? (HALLOWEEN)

Object: To avoid being cast under the witch's spell.

Equipment: None.

Description:

Players spread out across the gym or playing field. On the signal, the players walk around slowly. The teacher whispers to one student that he or she is the witch. (Eyes can be closed while the teacher whispers or the teacher can pretend to whisper to many students.) When the teacher shouts "Which Witch?," the players begin asking one another, "Are you the witch?" If the player asked is the witch, the witch winks at the player. This means that the player is under the witch's spell and also becomes a witch. If two witches wink at each other, they both are transformed into mere mortals. After a predetermined time, stop the game and count to see if there are more witches or more mortals.

FRANKEN-FIND (HALLOWEEN)

Object: To find the most Frankenstein emblems and score the most points.

Equipment: Small pieces of green paper or cardboard with faces drawn on the fronts and point values listed on the backs.

Description:

Divide the class into teams. Before class, hide (and record where you hid) the "Frankensteins." On the signal, students try to find the hidden objects. After all are found, tally the points to determine the winner.

Variations:

1. Vary the pieces to fit the holiday.
2. Have students design their own playing pieces.

FIGURE 7-9. Sample Frankenstein piece

CRANBERRY CROSS (THANKSGIVING)

Object: To be the first team to pass the cranberries to all teammates.

Equipment: One spoon per person; one bowl per team; five cranberries per bowl.

PLAYERS WITH SPOONS

BOWL OF CRANBERRIES

FIGURE 7-10. Set-up for Cranberry Cross

Description:

Divide the class into equal squads in shuttle formation. Start with one cranberry on a spoon. On the signal, the first player runs to the opposite line and gives the cranberry to the next player. This continues until all players return to their original spots and sit. The last player must put the berry back into the bowl before sitting. The first team to finish gets one point. Next, follow the same procedure using two cranberries on a spoon and award two points to the winner and so on, up to five cranberries on a spoon and five points to the winner. The squad with the most points at the end is declared the winner.

TURKEY TRAP (THANKSGIVING)

Object: To avoid being trapped by the turkey hunters.

Equipment: A drum or pot, and spoon.

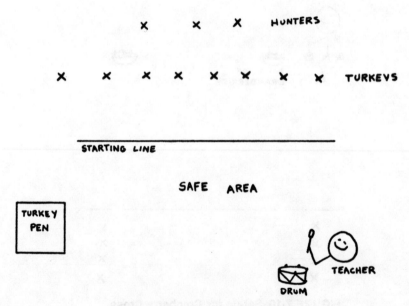

FIGURE 7-11. Turkey Trap set-up

Description:

Designate three players as the turkey hunters. On a signal, the remaining players (turkeys) follow the hunters in a single line, shoulder to shoulder. When the teacher bangs the drum or hits the pot, the hunters try to tag as many of the turkeys as possible before they get to the safe area. The trapped turkeys must go to the turkey pen and the game continues. The turkeys remain trapped for one turn and then are released. Alternate hunters with the turkeys so that each player has a chance to be a hunter.

SHOVEL THE SIDEWALK (WINTER)

Object: To be the first team to shovel the sidewalk.

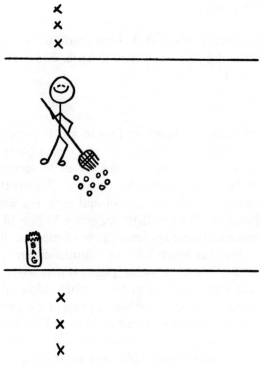

FIGURE 7-12. Shovel the Sidewalk set-up

Equipment: Small pieces of white styrofoam packing material; one push broom or regular broom per line; one paper bag per line.

Description:

Divide the class into teams of equal size in shuttle formations. The first player in each line is given a broom and a small pile of packing pieces. On the signal, the player sweeps the "snow" to the next player who then continues. The second player may not start until all the pieces have crossed the restraining line. The last player sweeps the snow back to the first and then puts all the pieces in a paper bag. The first team done is the winner.

HANUKKAH TREASURE HUNT (HANUKKAH)

Object: To accumulate points while trying to find the treasure by following clues.

Equipment: Cardboard Hanukkah clue cards with point values listed on the back (see Figure 7-13); index cards; pencils.

Description:

Divide the class into teams of four to six. Players must work together to find the hidden Hanukkah clue cards (hide the cards before class) and piece together the clues to determine the whereabouts of the *imaginary* hidden treasure. (Rather than hide a real treasure somewhere in the school and have students leaving class, we've found it works well to suggest a hiding place for an imaginary treasure and have students guess where that place might be.) Once the team has assembled its information and believes it has determined the treasure's hiding place, it may write that guess on an index card and submit it to the teacher. After all cards are submitted, the teacher reveals the hiding place of the treasure. The team with the correct answer receives points. If more than one team is correct, the one that submitted the correct answer first is the winner. Teams must make specific guesses as to the where-

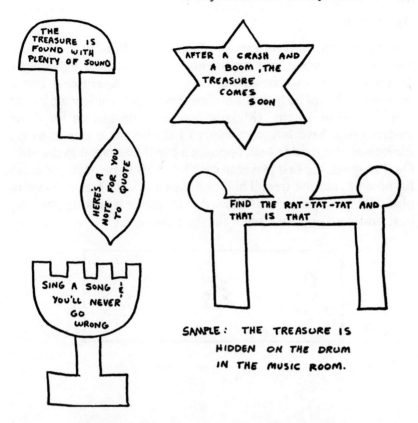

FIGURE 7-13. Hanukkah Treasure-Hunt clue cards

abouts of the treasure. To say the treasure is "in the gym" is not sufficient. They should say that the treasure is "in the gym behind the set of bleachers nearest the girls' locker room."

Duplicate cards can be hidden. Try to hide ten to twenty cards to give all teams an equal chance.

DECORATE THE TREE (CHRISTMAS)

Object: To decorate the tree in the prescribed manner.

Equipment: One construction paper or cardboard tree per line; paper ornaments; tape.

Description:

Divide the class into teams of equal size. Prior to this lesson, have students make tree ornaments out of paper or lightweight material. (They must be able to be taped to a paper tree.) These ornaments should be brought to class. Hand each student a piece of tape for his ornament. (Make a few extra ornaments for those students who have forgotten theirs.) Line up the teams in single file behind the starting line, opposite a paper tree taped to the wall. On the signal, the first player in each line runs to the tree and tapes his ornament to the tree. This continues until all ornaments are in place. Points or prizes can be awarded for the best looking tree, the best ornament, the first team finished and so on.

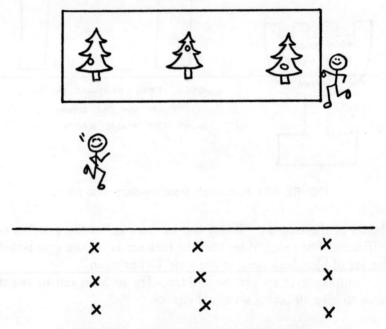

FIGURE 7-14. Set-up for Decorate the Tree

ALL TIED UP (CHRISTMAS)

Object: To be the first set of partners to wrap the "present."

Equipment: Wrapping paper or newspaper; tape; ribbon or yarn; blindfolds; one shoe box for each pair.

Description:

Divide the class into pairs. Designate one partner as wrapper and one as director. The wrapper puts on a blindfold and on the signal is directed to wrap the present. Points can be awarded for the best wrapped present, the funniest, the first done and so on. Partners then change roles.

Variation:

Eliminate the blindfolds and have partners cooperate to wrap the present using only their nondominant hands.

SANTA RELAY (CHRISTMAS)

Object: to construct a Santa Claus face more quickly and accurately than the opponents.

Equipment: Envelopes filled with cut-out cardboard Santa Claus pieces; masking tape.

Description:

Cut out Santa Claus pieces and place them in an envelope. Give one envelope to each team. At the signal, each player is to place one piece on the wall, return, and tag the next person. This continues until all pieces are up. Once taped to the wall, no piece can be rearranged. At the conclusion, points can be awarded for the first, second, and third groups done, and for the best-looking Santa.

Variations:

1. Use this same idea for other holidays and construct turkeys, pumpkins, witches, flags, and so on.
2. Allow students to design their own figures.

THE TWELVE DAYS OF CHRISTMAS (CHRISTMAS)

Object: To act out the gifts given on the Twelve Days of Christmas.

Equipment: Five gold or yellow hoops; any other equipment chosen by students for acting out the gifts.

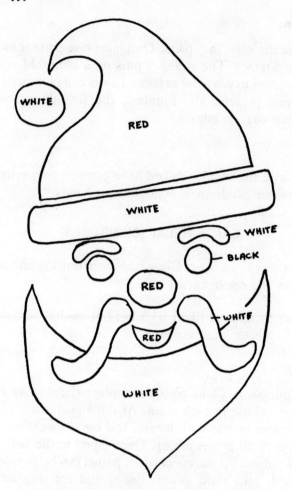

WHITE

RED

WHITE

WHITE

BLACK

RED

WHITE

RED

WHITE

FIGURE 7-15. Sample Santa Claus pieces

Description:

Have the class form a large circle. Ask for volunteers to be the actors and actresses. For example, you'll need one student to be the partridge in the pear tree, two to be the turtle doves, three to be the French hens, four calling birds, five golden rings (hoops), six geese-a-laying, seven swans-a-swimming, eight maids-a-milking, nine ladies dancing. ten lords-a-leaping, eleven pipers piping and twelve drummers drumming. Depending on the size of the class, some students may have to play several parts. Once every student is assigned a part, have the class sing the song "The Twelve Days of Christmas." Any time someone's part is mentioned, that person must run to the center of the circle and perform. For example, if the four calling birds are mentioned, the four students assigned that part run to the center, call out and imitate calling birds and then immediately return to their places while the next group runs out. We've found this to be a very enjoyable activity for all involved.

Variation:

Assign parts a few days ahead of time and allow students to design costumes at home. Award small prizes such as candy canes for the best performance and the best costume.

RACE FOR THE NEW YEAR (NEW YEAR)

Object: To be the first team to retrieve the card with the number of the new year written on it.

Equipment: Index cards with different years written on them in sequence; hula hoops.

Description:

Divide the class into teams of equal size. A stack of cards is placed at the end of each line. The cards are shuffled and placed face down and each team is informed of the number on the starting card (or year). On a signal, the first player for each team races to the end of the line and turns over cards until that first card is found. When that player's card is found, she must turn it face up and place it in her team's scoring zone (hula hoop) in sequential order. The player then returns to his/her line and tags the next player who must find the next year. After finding each year, the remaining cards must be returned to their face-down position before the next teammate is tagged. Play continues until one team has all the years placed in the hoop in sequential order, and holds up the New Year Card. The more cards, the more difficult the game.

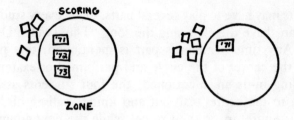

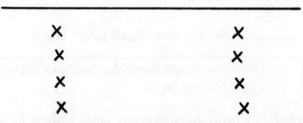

FIGURE 7-16. Set-up for Race for the New Year

Variation:

Have the team that retrieves the New Year Card first, run to a predetermined spot and raise the card by attaching it to a clip on a string, and pulling it up á la Times Square at midnight.

BOWL GAME TICKET MANIA (NEW YEAR)

Object: To be the team with the most bowl game tickets at the end of the game.

Equipment: Eight coffee cans (or bowls); two "safe deposit boxes" (shoebox with a slit in the lid); tickets (made from cardboard or construction paper); six pinnies (two different colors).

Description:

Divide the class into two equal teams. Each team has four ticket booths (tin coffee cans). One booth is for the Sugar Bowl, one for the Rose Bowl, one for the Orange Bowl, and one for the Cotton Bowl. Each can is filled with an equal number of tickets. Each team starts on its own half of the basketball court (or field) using the mid-court line as the divider. Each team designates three of its members as ushers who guard the tin cans. These guards must wear pinnies and must remain on their own half of the court.

All other players are spectators who are trying to get tickets to the bowl games. The spectators must go into the opponents' court and get a ticket out of one of the four tin cans and get back to their side before being tagged by an usher. Once a player has crossed into the opponents' territory, he is fair game unless he is standing in the

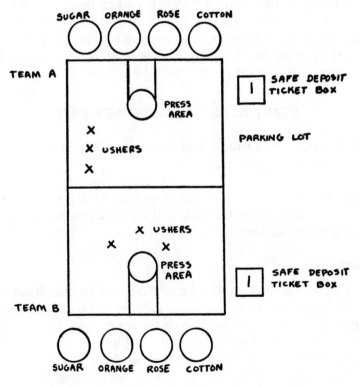

FIGURE 7-17. Set-up for Bowl Game Ticket Mania

press circle where he is **safe** (the circle around the top of the foul lane).

If a player is tagged by an usher while not in the press circle, she must go to the parking lot and remain there. If that player has a ticket, it must be given to the usher who returns it to the cans. Once a player has an opponent's ticket, it must be taken back to her team's side and placed in the safe deposit box (shoebox). The first team to get all of the opponents' bowl game tickets is the winner; or a time-limit game can be devised whereby the team with the most tickets after a pre-set time is the winner.

Variation:

Every member of each team has a ticket (they can be color coded to match the tin can in which they must be placed) and must go to the opposite team's ticket booths (cans) and deposit them. If a player is tagged by an opponent's usher while doing so, he or she must go to the parking lot. If a player is successful in depositing the ticket, he or she also sits down in the parking lot. After all players are in the parking lot, the team that has deposited the most tickets in the opponents' booths is declared the winner.

HEART TO HEART (VALENTINE'S DAY)

Object: To find your partner and get to the safety zone faster than other sets of partners.

Equipment: One paper heart per player (each heart has a word or number on the back that matches another heart); two paper bags.

Description:

Players are each given a paper heart and on the signal must find their matched partner without talking. Once two players pair up they must walk (or run, hop, leap, jump, skip, gallop) to the safety zone, arms hooked at the elbow. The last set to match up collects the hearts in the paper bags and the game begins again.

Pairs can be matched by animal names, numbers, math problems, spelling words, sports team names, symbols, or any other combinations.

FIGURE 7-18. Sample cards for Heart to Heart

Variation:

When using animal or sports cards, players must find their partners by imitating the particular animal or sport without talking.

BE MY VALENTINE

Object: To avoid being caught by the "valentine."

Equipment: A construction paper or cardboard valentine.

Description:

All the students stand in a circle with their hands together behind their backs, forming a "mailbox." The mail person with the valentine skips in a circle and places the valentine in one of the mailboxes. The valentine receiver then chases the mail person who must get back to the empty spot before being caught. If caught, the mail person remains the same. If not caught, the mail person joins the circle, the valentine receiver becomes the mail person, and the game continues.

FEBRUARY FLING (FEBRUARY EVENTS AND BIRTHDAYS)

Object: To complete the obstacle course that relates to famous events and birthdays in February faster than opponents.

Equipment: Two burlap sacks with both ends opened to form a tube; twelve cones; two plastic bats or sticks; manila folders; two Indian clubs; two pens; one globe (if not available, any round ball will do); two shoeboxes with slits in the tops; one container or bag of play money (bingo chips, pennies, slugs, or cardboard circles are fine)—have enough for each member of the class; two light bulbs cut out of cardboard; three hula hoops; masking tape; one cut-out heart per person.

Description:

Although this obstacle course may take a bit of extra preparation, it can serve as a valuable history lesson as well as a physical activity, and lends itself to further class discussion. For added emphasis, posters can be placed at each station depicting the date as well as the event. Divide the class in half once the obstacle course has been set up, as shown in Figure 7-19. On the signal, the first player from each team completes the course, then tags the next person in line until all players have completed the course. The first team to have all the players return is the winner. If a station is done incorrectly or missed, it must be done over.

Variation:

Have the teams compete against the clock rather than against each other.

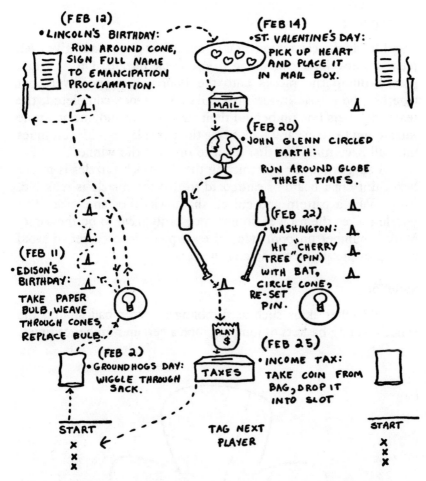

(FEB 12)
• LINCOLN'S BIRTHDAY: RUN AROUND CONE, SIGN FULL NAME TO EMANCIPATION PROCLAMATION.

(FEB 14)
• ST. VALENTINE'S DAY: PICK UP HEART AND PLACE IT IN MAIL BOX.

MAIL

(FEB 20)
• JOHN GLENN CIRCLED EARTH: RUN AROUND GLOBE THREE TIMES.

(FEB 22)
• WASHINGTON: HIT "CHERRY TREE" (PIN) WITH BAT, CIRCLE CONE, RE-SET PIN.

(FEB 11)
• EDISON'S BIRTHDAY: TAKE PAPER BULB, WEAVE THROUGH CONES, REPLACE BULB.

(FEB 2)
• GROUNDHOGS DAY: WIGGLE THROUGH SACK.

PLAY $

TAXES

(FEB 25)
• INCOME TAX: TAKE COIN FROM BAG, DROP IT INTO SLOT

START
x
x
x

TAG NEXT PLAYER

START
x
x
x

FIGURE 7-19. Set-up and description of February Fling Obstacle Course

SHAMROCK SHAKE-UP (ST. PATRICK'S DAY)

Object: To put together the shamrock puzzle and complete the designated tasks faster than the opponents.

Equipment: One large shamrock puzzle (made from green cardboard and cut into pieces) per team; one large envelope per team to hold the pieces; one hoop per team; one cone per team.

Description:

Divide the class into teams of up to four players and give each team an envelope containing a shamrock puzzle. On a signal, players dump the pieces onto the floor and cooperatively put together the puzzle inside their hula hoop. Once completed, the team members line up behind their starting line and one at a time run around the cone and back to tag the next player. This continues until all have run. The first team to finish is the winner.

A suggestion for constructing the shamrock puzzles is to use heavy-duty mat board or cardboard so that the puzzle is reusable. Also, make a pattern and cut all shamrocks the same size. The puzzle pieces themselves do not necessarily have to be the same. Mark a number on *both* sides of each piece in each set to avoid mixing of puzzle pieces among the sets.

Variation:

Add other skills such as dribbling a soccer ball around the cone, shooting baskets or jumping rope a certain number of times.

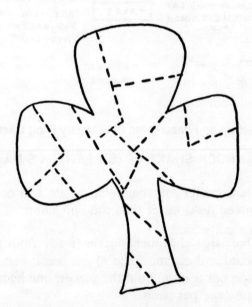

FIGURE 7-20. Sample Shamrock puzzle

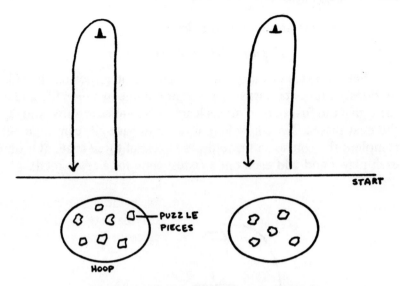

FIGURE 7-21. Set-up for Shamrock Shake-Up

TRICK-TRACK MEET (APRIL FOOLS' DAY)

Object: To complete the tricks and challenges more quickly or more accurately than the opponents.

Equipment: Cardboard boxes of various heights (paint turtles on the sides if desired and call them the high and low turtles); hula hoop; frisbees; one unpeeled banana per team; one balloon per person; one scorecard per team; pencils; stopwatches.

Description:

Divide the class into four teams of equal size, and start each team at a different event. Teams compete against the clock and all times or points are added together to get a team score for each event. Rotate the teams until all four teams have been at all four events. When all teams have finished all the events, compare score cards and award three points for a first place finish, two for a second, and one for a third for each event. The team with the highest point total is declared the trick-track meet winner.

The events are described below:

Event 1: High and Low Turtles

Set up boxes of various heights and paint turtles on the sides (optional). Students start at the restraining line in single file and on the signal the first person runs, clears each hurdle, returns, and tags the next player. Time how long it takes to have all team members complete the course and record the fastest of three trials. (Or time each player and add each one's fastest time for a team total).

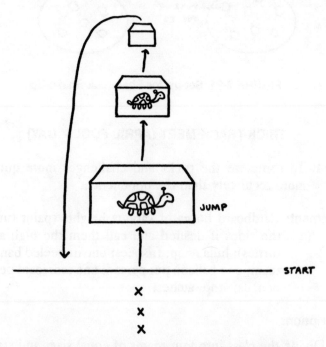

FIGURE 7-22. Set-up for High and Low "Turtles"

Event 2: Banana Pass Relay

This can be done around a track or in shuttle line formation. Rather than passing a baton, team members pass a banana. Record the fastest time of three trials.

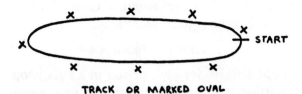

FIGURE 7-23. Set-up for Banana Pass Relay

Event 3: Spot Put

Set up the hula hoops as shown in Figure 7-24. Each team member gets one chance to toss the frisbee (or beanbags, tin pie plate, cardboard circle, eraser) into the hoops. Assign each hoop a

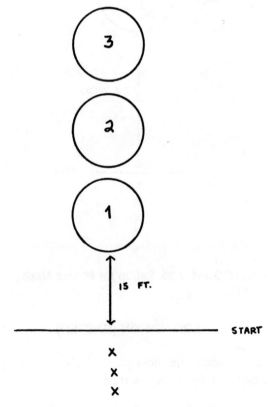

FIGURE 7-24. Set-up for Spot Put

point value and add the scores together. Give all teams three trials to come up with their highest point total.

Event 4: 50-Yard Mash

Place one balloon for each person in a hula hoop fifty yards from the starting line. On the signal, the first person runs fifty yards to the hoop, takes a balloon (they can be blown up or the student can do it then), mashes it with his feet until it pops, dashes back, and tags the next player and so on until all players have had a turn. Time the event to see how long it takes all players to perform this task. Record the time.

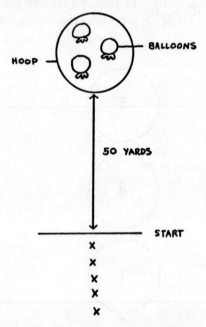

FIGURE 7-25. Set-up for 50-Yard Mash

EGG 'EM ON (EASTER)

Object: To accumulate the most points by successfully completing the tasks in the time allotted.

Equipment: (Varies with the tasks designed.) Ten plastic eggs (the type that pantyhose comes in or store-bought colored eggs); strips of paper with the times "five seconds," "ten seconds," "fifteen seconds," or "twenty seconds" printed on them (place the strips inside the various eggs at random); one task list per team; stopwatches; scorecards and pencils.

Description:

Divide the class into four or more teams of equal size and give each team a task list. Place the plastic eggs containing the times in the front of the room or gymnasium. The first player from each team looks over the task sheet and announces which task the team will attempt and its point value. After all players have announced their chosen tasks, they go to the front of the room and choose a plastic egg. They then open the egg to discover the time in which they must complete the task. If the task is completed within the allotted time, that person scores the points for her team. To keep track of time, a timer calls out "Ready, Go!" and then announces out loud, "five seconds, ten seconds, etc."

The time aspect adds a new strategy to the game because it may be too difficult to do a five-point task in only five seconds and the player would receive no points. The team with the most points after a pre-set number of rounds is the winner. Here are some sample challenges and point values (challenges can be adapted to different physical education units when desired):

One Point
three jumping jacks
one forward roll
three sit-ups
run up to cone and back
three chest passes against wall

Two Points
five jumping jacks
two backward rolls
five sit-ups
dribble ball to cone and back
hop to nearby cone and back

Three Points
eight jumping jacks
hold a handstand the
entire time
eight push-ups
run weaving in and out of
cones and back
hit a tennis ball against wall
five times

Four Points
ten jumping jacks
ten push-ups
dribble ball to basket and
score a basket
five cartwheels in a row
dribble a soccer ball and
score a goal

<u>Five Points</u>
twenty jumping jacks
fifteen push-ups
score three baskets
dribble ball weaving in and out of cones and score a basket
sprint the entire length of the gym and back
jump rope fifteen times

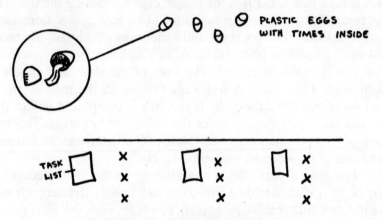

FIGURE 7-26. Set-up for Egg 'Em On

Variations:

1. If a player announces that he can do the challenge in half
   the time that he picked, the point values are doubled if the
   player is successful. This must be announced before
   picking an egg.
2. Have students design their own challenges and assess point
   values.

BUNNY TAG (EASTER)

Object: To avoid being tagged by an Easter bunny.

Equipment: Wrestling mat or area marked with boundaries; one ball
(any size) per person or large rubber strips or bands cut
from old inner tubes; one large box or ball bag.

Description:

   Two or three students are picked to be Easter bunnies to start the game. Other players start in a designated spot touching the Easter bunnies. On a signal, the bunnies hop (actually jump) toward the players while holding a ball between their knees (or strap an inner tube band around their knees) and attempt to tag the other players. If tagged, that player must get a ball (or band) from the box and become a bunny. If a player steps out of bounds he or she automatically becomes a bunny. Play continues until one player is left and that player starts the next game as the Easter bunny.

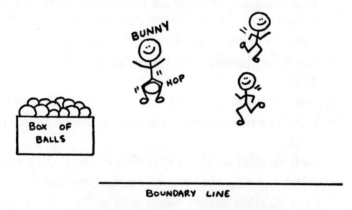

BOUNDARY LINE

FIGURE 7-27. Set-up for Bunny Tag

STARS AND STRIPES (MEMORIAL DAY)

Object: To be the first team to accumulate thirteen stars on its flag.

Equipment: Star task cards (other equipment will vary according to the activities chosen).

Description:

   Divide the class into teams of equal size. Alternating players from each team come to the flag to choose a star task card. The star cards are worth from one to four stars. The card is read aloud to all teams. The team that chooses the card tries to accomplish the task it describes before the other teams do. If successful, the choosing team receives the number of stars on the card. If the other teams finish first, they cannot receive the stars but are rewarded by having successfully blocked their opponents.

Sample star activities include:

1. One person travels through the legs of all of her teammates. (one star)

2. All hop on one foot and form a circle. (two stars)

3. All teammates join to form a large letter "M." (three stars)

4. Crab walk from one end of the gym to the other. (four stars)

5. Both teams start on the same line. Each member of a team takes one giant step past the previous member. The team farthest ahead is the winner. (three stars)

6. Form the letters "H," then "Q." (four stars)

7. Pass a ball between the legs of all team members. (two stars)

8. Join hands and travel from Point A to Point B. (two stars)

9. Make ten team baskets, counting each one aloud. (four stars)

10. Each member leapfrogs over all the others. (four stars)

11. Select and sing one verse of a song. (two stars)

12. Each member shakes hands with all the others. (three stars)

Once a team has accumulated thirteen stars, that team is declared the winner.

Variation:

Allow the students to design their own challenges and assess the point values.

8

I Can't Wait to Go to Gym Today

Motivational Ideas to
Keep Your Students Enthused
About Physical Education

Our purpose in writing this book has been to help you hear "I can't wait to go to Gym today," from every one of your students. We are confident that you will get this type of reaction when you incorporate games and activities that are included in the first seven chapters of this book. There are over three hundred different resource ideas and materials from which to choose those that are appropriate for your program. The key to keeping your students motivated is to provide challenge and variety in all facets of your program. This is just as important for the five year old as for the fourteen year old. With this in mind, we have provided games and activities for all elementary grade levels. Even more important, we have provided ideas and suggestions that will make it possible for you to modify and change the games and activities to make them applicable to different age and skill levels.

This chapter supplements the ideas and materials included in the first seven chapters. It is also used to emphasize methodology and instructional techniques. The introduction and explanation of a game is just as important in stimulating student interest as are the activities themselves. The Change-of-Pace chapter (Chapter 5) also provides excellent ideas on teaching strategies and every chapter includes tips to help make your teaching more effective as you broaden the scope of your program with the innovative games and activities.

Let's take another look at some ways that you can motivate your students and make their physical education class the highlight of their day.

MUSIC

Music is a universal language. All children enjoy music. Naturally, the type of music that your students like will vary with their ages. Cultural and geographical influences also determine the kinds of music that you will find most effective. It should be remembered that skillful use of music can be one of your most valuable teaching aids, and there are many different ways that music can be used. Chapter 3 presents rhythms that you can teach, showing ways that music is used as a focus when teaching physical education activities. Every program should include a component devoted to dance and rhythms. There is an innate desire on the part of all children to dance. This is true whether the child's movement can be categorized as a specific dance or not.

There are many other ways that music can be used in your physical education program. Music has the capacity to pick up the tempo in a class and generate student excitement. An otherwise slow lesson can be turned around with musical accompaniment. Bring to class music that complements the activity or game that you are using. Use this music as background music during your class. Vary the volume to stimulate additional enthusiasm and to make it possible to communicate verbally with the members of the class when giving directions or changing the class emphasis. Background music can be used to soothe or to excite. Select your music to serve your objective.

Music is ideal for your class warm-ups, both structured and nonstructured. In a structured format the music should be planned to set the tempo for the warm-up routine that is used, to keep the class moving and make the warm-up lively and enjoyable. Another good way to use music is to tape verbal instructions and directions to music. This frees the teacher for other class responsibilities or for working with students on an individual basis.

Music is also great when using an unstructured warm-up format. Simply select different music daily and let your students design their individual warm-ups by moving to the music. Another possibility is to have students lead the warm-up and have the rest of the class mimic their movements.

Another effective way to get your students involved through music is to let them bring their favorite music to class for exercising, movement exploration, a pantomine session or for some other activity that is planned for physical education. When students have a hand in creating the climate for the class, their interest level immediately jumps upward.

Instructional records and tapes can also be a fine addition to a teacher's repertoire. Most companies that specialize in physical education music have records and tapes of this type. They can be excellent in teaching new activities and increasing the scope of your physical education program.

Also, let your students make their own music. One way is to improvise instruments for them to use, and another is to use the skills of children who play instruments. Call upon your music teacher for assistance and suggestions. Better yet, make this aspect of your program a joint project with your school's music department.

MEDIA

Different uses of media materials have been mentioned in other chapters of this book. Suffice it to say that the innovative teacher will make extensive use of various forms of audio-visual materials and equipment. The previous section pointed out different uses of record players, tape recorders, and the tapes and records that are available. Our first book, *What Are We Doing in Gym Today?** provided many different activities to use with an overhead projector.

Newspapers and magazines can be rich resources for a physical education class. Many action pictures of athletes capture the joy and excitement of movement and can be used effectively for bulletin boards and wall displays. Children can mimic the actions portrayed through pictures. Photographs found in papers can be brought to class by your students. When you have a basketball unit, have them bring pictures relating to that activity. They can point out important playing techniques that are shown in the pictures, describe the action that they see in the pictures, or simply use their pictures to form a collage to heighten interest in the basketball unit.

There are many different types of films that are available for use in class. Used judiciously, they can be very effective in

*Kenneth G. Tillman and Patricia Rizzo Toner. *What Are We Doing in Gym Today?* (West Nyack, NY: Parker Publishing Co., Inc., 1983).

motivating your students. Films are excellent to show students skilled performers. What better way to motivate students in a gymnastic class than to show a film of an Olympic performer in action? In addition to sixteen millimeter and eight millimeter films, many super eight films are available. Variable speed loop films are perfect for use when teaching a new skill. They allow students to observe the skill numerous times while interspersing their practice with observation of the film. Loop films are also excellent for individualizing instruction, for using task cards, and for setting up teaching stations. This can be very valuable to the teacher who has a large class with varied skill levels. Loop films can be an important aid in letting the students progress at their own pace.

Videotapes are an important motivational as well as instructional aid. Videotapes showing proper execution of individual skills or an entire activity can be used just as effectively as loop films for instructional purposes. Children like to see themselves on the screen. Videotape is ideal to film children in action. To view themselves performing in an activity is a surefire method of motivating students in a class. Equally important is the use of videotape to make it possible for students to see themselves performing a skill or participating in an activity and then to make corrections based on having seen their performances on the tapes.

Videotaping has another valuable motivational use. It can be used to build a library of special lessons. Search out colleagues or students who have strengths in different areas. Use their unique talents by having them tape lessons that you can use for your classes. Having surprise teachers periodically is a helpful motivational device.

Don't overlook the opportunity to let your students make their own films or videotapes. They can make a tape that depicts activities that they covered in class, or they can make a tape that will show another class how to perform a new sport. There are many other possibilities for using film making as a motivational device in your classes. For example, let your class make a tape of a folk dance that it is doing or have students make up a dance that they think typifies a culture they are studying in class. They can then use this tape in their classroom. Films or tapes made in class can also be used for public relations purposes in the school and in the community. The effect is heightened when students comment on the tape as it is being run.

STUDENT DESIGNED GAMES

Too often, we not only fail to utilize the skills of our students, but also we fail to stimulate their creative abilities. One of the best ways to encourage creativity is to involve students in the design of games that are used in class. In addition to being a fine motivational technique, it also serves as a rich source of exciting new games encompassing the elements of surprise, challenge, fun and variety.

It is best to provide guidance to get your students started in designing games. One of the best foundations for them to build on is your setting an example by designing games that are used in class. Determine your class objectives and make up a game or games that will make it possible for your students to attain these objectives. One technique is to start with a familiar game and modify it to meet your class needs. A difficult hurdle to overcome with older children is changing their attitudes about traditional games. They have been taught that there is one way to play each game. This is true for both informal activities like relays, and for structured games like softball. By changing the way some of their traditional games are played, they will see that there are different ways that any game can be played. It is then a much easier step to designing completely new games.

The next logical phase in the game designing process is for the teacher to work with students in making up a game. This guidance helps students succeed if they have never tried to develop a game before. If they are experienced in participating in a game designing process, it doesn't matter if some of their games are not successful. They simply make further changes or modifications and try the game again. However, if they have never tried to make up a game, initial failure can cause them to become discouraged and perhaps to lose confidence in their abilities. As a teacher, you may want to establish the safety rules, and perhaps indicate the skills that will be used in the game. Let your students decide how the game will be started, what the scoring system will be, what equipment will be used, and what penalties will be needed. You will be the facilitator as the game is being developed. The amount of assistance that you provide will be determined by the ages of your students and their previous experience. Let them experiment as they are developing the game so they will see any aspect that is not workable rather than your telling them that some element won't work.

It is suggested that they initially work in groups. They can start out by modifying a game that they have played, and gradually design new games that may be combinations of two or more games, or may contain the elements of several games. With this experience, they are then ready to design totally new games. Naturally, any new game will contain locomotor and/or ball handling skills that are found in other games.

When starting to design games it is helpful if the teacher provides some parameters. For example, the teacher may ask for games that have two players and then three players. Perhaps the next step would be a game for six players and eventually a game for two large teams. The teacher may also provide the equipment around which a game can be designed. One group of students may be given a soccer ball, a wiffle ball bat and three cones. They use these pieces of equipment in a game. The teacher can stipulate the skills that are to be included—kicking with the nondominant foot, for example, or throwing underhanded or skipping.

The final step is to let each individual design his own game. The teacher is available for assistance and to check the games for safety, but otherwise the students are on their own. Students are able to come up with fantastic games.

New games should be played by all members of the class. Posting the names of the new games and the names of the game designers on the wall or bulletin board adds to the excitement and further motivates the students. There are many ways that these student-designed games can be used in your class. You can use one at the start of each class. You can have a unit devoted to student games. You can use them periodically for a change of pace. The students can use them before school or during their lunch periods if time and facilities permit. Suffice it to say that student-designed games will be a stimulating experience for students in your program and are a fine way to increase interest in physical education and spark student creativity.

LEARNING CENTERS

The term "learning center," as used in this section, is used to refer to both individual teaching stations and to the learning environment that is established in your gymnasium through individualized stations. Learning centers are not only excellent instructional tools but also can be equally valuable from a motivational standpoint. It is possible to challenge all skill levels and truly individualize instruction with a physical education program that makes liberal use of learning centers. Learning centers can be placed throughout the gymnasium. You can also make use of library and media center facilities to increase the scope of your learning centers.

Create a series of stations throughout your teaching facility. Use a teaching aid at each station to show what skill is to be covered at that station. The teaching aid may be a loop film, overhead projector, tape recorder or simply a poster placed at the station. The students review the skill that is being shown, and then practice that skill at that learning center. A progression of skills should be demonstrated at the learning center so students can proceed at their own pace. They never need to wait for another student who is progressing at a slower speed. Appropriate equipment is placed at each station in your learning center.

Task cards can also be used effectively at each station. When students go to a station they check the task card and progress from the easy to the difficult tasks. Students have their own progress cards which the instructor uses when checking student skills. Peer evaluation can also be used effectively. An advantage of a learning center of this type is that the teacher is free to move from station to station to assist and encourage the students.

A variation you might want to incorporate in your learning center would be to have students answer questions about techniques or activities that are included at a station. Material can be provided at each station or you can have information learning centers set up in the library or media center. The students would then go to that area to research their questions before returning to the gymnasium center to practice the skill.

The students can rotate from station to station on a scheduled basis or you can let them select a station at each class and move from station to station when they are ready. The amount of flexibility that is provided will depend on the size of the class, the number of individual learning centers that are available, and the experience your students have had working independently.

Your learning center can be set up for any unit you are covering. Gymnastic skills fit very nicely into a station format but the skills of any sport or activity can be included just as effectively. Sometimes students need to work in groups of two or three. For example, practicing a volleyball set works best with three students. Learning centers can include small areas or large areas. One-half of the gym might be used for one station when the assigned task is to incorporate the basketball skills that have been learned into a game situation.

Learning centers can be an important means of motivating students by helping provide a varied curriculum that challenges each student to work up to his or her potential. Every curriculum needs to be organized so that students will be able to progress toward increased utilization of their knowledge and abilities. Students need to be challenged to maintain interest and to insure personal growth through physical education.

SIMULATION

Children love to mimic life situations. One way that the innovative teacher can capitalize on this love is to model class activities on real situations and let the children act out the real life activity. This is what simulations are all about. The activity allows the children to imagine that they are really experiencing some activity such as searching through a jungle or trying to capture a wild pony. Younger children love to have a story read to them and pretend that they are really experiencing the activities in the story. Records or tapes can also be used effectively for this purpose.

Lead-up games and skill drills also should make extensive use of simulation. Children are easily motivated when participating in lead-up games if the lead-up imitates the real game, and patterning a skill drill after the real game greatly increases interest.

Older students are motivated when they have the opportunity to simulate the performance of their sports heroes while participating in physical education games. Structuring your games to provide for this kind of expression adds an important dimension to your physical education program.

Another way to make use of simulations for older students is to set up various game situations. For example, in a basketball unit, set up a hypothetical situation in which one team trails by one point with ten seconds left in the game. Give the ball to the team that is behind and see if it can win the game. Similar situations can be set up for almost every other game. Simulations of this type are used extensively by coaches. Physical educators should take a leaf from their notebooks and use this valuable instructional and motivational tool.

Machines that make use of the principle of simulation can also be used extensively to provide motivation. Softball and baseball pitching machines and tennis machines are excellent examples. However, you don't have to have funds for expensive machines in order to use this kind of simulation in your physical education program. The innovative teacher will design home-made rackets for racket sports and improvise field markings and game implements for other sports to allow students to simulate regular games or components of games.

Simulations can add an important ingredient to a physical education program. They make it easier to motivate children because activities become more realistic and meaningful. Simulations also make it possible to increase student participation by increasing the amount of activity time each student has during a class period.

TEACHING TECHNIQUES

Varying your teaching approach can be an important aid in maintaining a stimulating classroom environment and keeping your students motivated. The same content will look different if presented differently. Sameness is one thing that will eventually turn off every student. It is, of course, critical to have a comprehensive, challenging curriculum. This is the foundation of every successful program. This means that the program will contain something for everyone. Outdoor education, risk activities, dance, fitness activities, leisure sports, combatives, and team sports are examples of activity categories that should be included in a good physical education program. The outstanding physical education program has something in addition to a good curriculum—a teacher of good quality whose teaching techniques motivate students to involve themselves totally in the activities that the curriculum provides.

There isn't one best teaching approach or technique. The skilled teacher is able to use different techniques to meet individual and class differences. Sameness has a tendency to create boredom. This entire book has been keyed to new and different activities and different ways of involving students in physical education activities. This section contains some additional teaching techniques.

Mini-contracts can be used effectively for several physical education activities. Gymnastics and swimming contracts are particularly good. Give your students a sheet containing course requirements with additional options that the students can select. All students must meet certain specific skill requirements and then each may choose from a list of options of varying skill levels. Give each option a specific value. The more difficult the option, the higher the value. Mini-contracts of this type provide a challenge to the skilled student and often lure the less skilled to experiment with new stunts and activities.

Have your students make use of an activity rating scale. They rate the activity during the unit and give you their evaluation when the unit is completed. This motivational device keeps student interest and provides you with valuable information to assist you in varying your unit the next time you teach it. The rating scale must be written for the age level that is using it. Questions covering the number of skills learned, fitness attained, teaching approach, amount of time available to play and to work on skills, enjoyment, and challenge provided should be included. Consider having the students assist in designing the scale. This will increase their interest in this technique.

Periodically, let the class participate in activities that they completed earlier in the year. Doing this at the end of each quarter of the school year or at the end of each semester can create excitement and interest. You might devote one or more class periods to mini-sessions on each activity that has been covered, or incorporate the activities into a relay race/obstacle course. Skills learned in each activity would form the obstacles in the relay race, and students would have to demonstrate each skill that was included in the obstacle course before the next member of their relay team could start through the course. Another technique would be to run mini-tournaments using games from previous units. Competition would be timed to keep the activity within the time limit available.

Involve students in the establishment of objectives for your units. This helps them know what is expected during the course. Let students develop personal objectives. This can be a fine way to motivate students and it is an effective technique to use when individualizing your instruction.

Give participatory opportunities to students in your class. Even such things as dividing the class into groups and having them "sound off" during warm-ups can have a positive motivational effect. Another technique would be to involve your students in the teaching process. A seventh grader can be an effective aide for a kindergarten class, or a skilled sixth grade dancer can be used as a peer demonstrator and teacher. There are many other ways that you can involve your students as teachers. Work out procedures whereby students demonstrate to different classes or teach skills to a squad in their own classes.

Have your students study the why and how of an activity or sport. This can be an out-of-class assignment that they would then share with the rest of the class.

Bring "experts" to your class to demonstrate or teach. College athletes, community leaders, parents, and professional organizations are just some of the resources that should be tapped. Students can lead you to many good resources.

Refer to Chapter 5 (Change-of-Pace Ideas) for many more teaching technique ideas that will further motivate your students.

Throughout this book we have provided new and modified games and activities, together with different teaching approaches and ideas for physical education. We encourage you to use this material and information to keep your programs lively and your students motivated. We believe that every physical education program can nurture a child's natural love of movement and, we believe even more firmly, that no physical education program should stifle this love. This is the goal of every idea and activity in this book.

Index

225